HIGH PERFORMANCE
FENCING
THE SEVENTH ESSENTIAL

Leon Paul
Leon Paul
HATOEL
Maor
Leon Paul
London
F I E
FEDERATION
INTERNATIONALE
D'ESCRIME

HIGH PERFORMANCE
FENCING
THE SEVENTH ESSENTIAL

ED ROGERS
FOREWORD BY GEORGINA USHER

THE CROWOOD PRESS

First published in 2015 by
The Crowood Press Ltd
Ramsbury, Marlborough
Wiltshire SN8 2HR

www.crowood.com

© Ed Rogers 2015

All rights reserved. No part of this publication may be reproduced or transmitted in any form or by any means, electronic or mechanical, including photocopy, recording, or any information storage and retrieval system, without permission in writing from the publishers.

British Library Cataloguing-in-Publication Data
A catalogue record for this book is available from the British Library.

ISBN 978 1 84797 985 8

Frontispiece: Leon Paul Cup, Men's Individual Foil Semi-final, London, 2013. Kristjan Archer of Great Britain, left, fights Maor Hatoel of Israel. Hatoel won 15/7 and went on to win gold, beating Italy's Tobia Biondo 15/12 in the final. (Photo: Graham Morrison)

Dedication
This book is dedicated to my wonderful wife Hilary.

Acknowledgements
Thanks to Dr Paolo Colombani at the Swiss Forum for Sports Nutrition for permission to reproduce its diagram 'Food Pyramid for Athletes'; to Jane Griffin for reading and commenting on the 'Nutrition' chapter; and Linlithgow Academy for permission to photograph on the premises. Graham Morrison's photographs appear as indicated. All other photographs and drawings are by the author.

Disclaimers
Please note that the author and the publisher of this book do not accept any responsibility whatsoever for any error or omission, nor any loss, injury, damage, adverse outcome or liability suffered as a result of the use of the information contained in this book, or reliance upon it. Since some of the training exercises can be dangerous and could involve physical activities that are too strenuous for some individuals to engage in safely, it is essential that a doctor be consulted before training is undertaken.

Typeset by Jean Cussons Typesetting, Diss, Norfolk

Printed and bound in India by Replika Press Pvt Ltd

CONTENTS

	Foreword by Georgina Usher, CEO of British Fencing	6
	Preface	7
	Introduction	9
Chapter 1	Fitness and Training	13
Chapter 2	Strength and Conditioning	35
Chapter 3	Nutrition	59
Chapter 4	Talent or Hard Work?	76
Chapter 5	Sports Psychology	88
Chapter 6	Becoming a High Performance Fencer	109
Chapter 7	The Seventh Essential (In Conclusion)	141
	Glossary	146
	References	151
	Index	157

FOREWORD

To get to the top in world fencing you must work incredibly hard, find an inspiring coach and choose high-quality sparring partners who can push you to your limits. In addition, you will need a never-ending supply of self-belief and motivation to overcome short-term setbacks and continue working towards your longer-term goals. As you approach the higher levels in the sport, the time spent training, travelling and competing can be life-consuming. You will have to balance the cycle of training and competition activities, necessary to reach peak performance, as well as find space for the other things that make life meaningful.

Lessons learned early in life have an enduring quality that can last a lifetime. From the earliest days in your fencing career, close attention to detail becomes dominant, along with a persevering quality you will need to keep going, even when training or fencing feels difficult and other problems arise. Above all, you must hold on to your love of the sport, seek out constantly ways to improve and never falter in the belief that one day you will succeed.

Beyond the fundamentals of learning to fence there are other factors that, although they may seem incidental at the start, are vital in achieving long-term success. World-class fencers need to stay remarkably fit. Fencing-specific fitness is also required, often achieved through formal strength and conditioning programmes, using specialist advice. The importance of good nutritional standards should also be understood. What you eat will have a direct bearing on how well you perform, how hard you train and how fast you recover. The role of psychology in sport has now risen in prominence to the extent that many fencers now include mental training as part of their regular weekly routines. These and other topics are introduced within the scope of this book and should provide invaluable points of reference for all.

Georgina Usher
CEO of British Fencing

As a competitor, Georgina Usher has been on the British team at eleven World Championships, has been an FIE World Cup medallist, Commonwealth Championships medallist and British Women's Épée Champion ten times.

PREFACE

> There are six essentials in a fencer's mind.
> The first is called spirit;
> The second, rhythm;
> The third, thought;
> The fourth, technique;
> The fifth, tactic,
> And the last is strategy.
>
> (Tau, 2005, p.12)

Six essentials have been described that are present in a fencer's mind. You can fight with indomitable spirit, experience the changing rhythms of a bout and think your way quickly around difficult problems. Indeed it has been said that: 'Fencing is a fascinating game co-ordinating the mind and body in a harmonious form of movement. It has often been linked to a game of chess played at lightning speed.' (de Beaumont, 1968, p.13) In this sense, there is not a move or action which cannot (potentially) be answered. This is an 'open skill' where individual moves are a means to winning. (Anderson, 1973) Technique is also of paramount importance: 'Technical versatility is the base of richness of tactics and enables the fencer to surprise his (/her) opponent, not only by speed and choice of time, but also by variety of action.' (Czajkowski, 2005, p.70)

Alaux (1975, p.172) says: 'Fencing as a sport is classified as a "finished skill" that requires both high speed and accuracy. Technique is defined as "the mechanical or formal part of an art". It allows the expression of one's potential at its highest level. Potential is determined by the quality of the fencer's senses, physical coordination, reflexes (both mental and physical), tactical ability, imagination, and so on. Undoubtedly, the foundation of a fencer begins with the development of his (/her) technique.'

Many factors are necessary to ensure effective fencing, some of which have been listed by Beke and Polgár (1963, p.28) as follows: 'physical adaptability, adequate technique, tactics, sense of distance and timing, good reflexes, psychological adaptability, diligence, will power, ability to survey situations quickly and to take decisions, the will to fight, the ability to observe, speed, dexterity, stamina, and of course, strength.' It has been observed that when applying tactics and strategy, two specific types of skill are in play: physical and mental. (Cross and Kirkham, 1996) Indeed 'To obtain the full satisfaction from fencing it is necessary to use one's brain as much as one's body.' (de Beaumont, 1954, p.13) In the words of Alaux (1975, p.171): 'Any muscular effort is as much a mental act as conversation or writing.'

Modern fencing is a highly competitive sport. Many complex physical and mental qualities are necessary in order to compete successfully; and the 'seventh essential' in a high-performance fencer's mind, is how to prepare him/herself physically and mentally to fence.

Preparation in this sense implies forethought; working to achieve a highly developed state of physical and mental readiness, in order to perform at one's best (in a sustained

PREFACE

manner) at a particular point in time. To achieve this, fencers are likely to consider various questions and find some answers: What is fitness and how should I train? What is strength and conditioning? What and when should I eat/drink, in order to perform best? Am I prepared to spend all the time (and money) necessary, to reach the top? Will thinking differently about myself and my opponents help me to succeed? What tactical applications will be of most value? Any individual's list could potentially be quite lengthy and diverse.

The following series of thoughts and observations are far from all-embracing, but does attempt to address some of these questions. They are an exploration of what it means to become, or to coach someone who wishes to become, a high-performance fencer.

My first book, *Fencing: Essential Skills Training* (The Crowood Press, 2003), was written in the form of a training manual of sorts and many of the photographs were taken by passing a camera round at a fencing club. *Advanced Fencing Techniques: Discussions with Bert Bracewell* (The Crowood Press, 2013), came about after I met Prof. Bert Bracewell at a fencing competition in Edinburgh. He had come across his notes of fencing lessons he had taken in the past, and wished to record the many fencing variations he had learned during his career; which then formed the basis of that book. Luckily, Bert was able to appear in a number of the photographs, depicting some of these actions. In this book, a number of (fencing-related) topics have been examined, in an attempt to get an overall picture of 'high performance' in the broader context of fencing skills. Most of the photographs that appear herein have been taken at fencing venues. I am grateful to all those who appear in these photographs for their tolerance and for the obvious enthusiasm they display.

For those readers in the United States and others who use numerical fencing terminology, I would ask for your indulgence later on when typical British terminology is used; the tactical variations described are what matters and I hope that this will in no way spoil your enjoyment. Also, I have attempted assiduously to avoid the use of the masculine term 'his', in isolation. The term 'High Performance Fencing' and the contents of this book, apply equally to men and women fencers.

Anyway, I hope you enjoy reading this book – good luck with your fencing.

Ed Rogers, Fife, Scotland

INTRODUCTION

Once their interest is captivated, people pursue fencing for the same reasons they pursue many other activities… These activities satisfy their need to use their abilities as significant, creative, self-reliant, and confident beings.
 (Garret, Kaidanov and Pezza, 1995, p.7)

Over the years, my interest in fencing has given me a great deal of satisfaction and I have no doubt that as an adult I am more confident as a result. It has been said that: 'Fencing develops quick thinking, powers of concentration, decision and self-discipline to a high degree. It gives poise, balance and muscular control, and is valuable for strengthening the limbs and back.' (de Beaumont, 1978, p.12). In combat, a fencer must balance wisdom with audacity, always being willing to take a 'reasonable' risk. (Campos, 1988) Just as chess is based on a limited number of moves that can be used with almost infinite combinations, fencing is also based on a limited number of moves. (Manley, 1979) Yet within these: 'Fencing provides a continuum of complexity and an unlimited range of mental stimulation, as the possible attacks and defences grow more and more involved and the moment of the final arrival of the touch becomes more and more delayed.' (Wyrick, 1971, p.6) In this vein, Anderson (1973, p.9) describes fencing as 'a game of physical chess, without checkmate, for there is not a fencing move or situation which cannot be answered'.

It is sometimes suggested that fencing develops one side of the body at the expense of the other. To some extent this is correct. An examination of the forearms of any regular fencer will show greater muscular development in the sword arm. This apparent lack of symmetry can be overcome by learning to fence with both hands but the fact that few ever do shows how little importance is placed on this. It is more important to remember that all parts of the body are exercised while fencing and the muscles of the abdomen, particularly, are kept in very good shape. (Hett, 1951)

Alaux (1975, p.183) underscores this point when he says: 'Fencing is an inherently asymmetrical sport. The rear leg and the front leg receive different stimuli. The hand holding the weapon and the hand in the rear have different functions. This can result in the disproportionate development of the stressed portions of the anatomy unless a general exercise program with symmetrical exercises is undertaken to develop the strength of both sides equally.'

It is important when setting out to become a fencer that you have a clear understanding of where you are going. If you have strong family support, perhaps a family member who takes a keen interest in your progress, providing moral (and perhaps financial) support and who may also accompany you to fencing competitions, this is bound to help. Some may be fortunate to have a parent who has fenced and who can explain how fencing

INTRODUCTION

competitions work, give helpful pointers and even to some extent provide early coaching. Alternatively, you must find support at a local fencing club.

At such clubs you will encounter a wide variety of personalities from different backgrounds, each with their own reason for taking up the sport. (Norcross, 1978) Indeed, a fencer's personality affects the style of fencing and tactics they adopt in competition. This is reflected in their personal motivation, level of arousal, and temperament. (Czajkowski, 2005)

Perhaps beginning with borrowed 'club kit', you will graduate to owning (and in time replacing) your own. Coaching, club facilities and kit all have to be paid for, as will entry fees and travel to and from fencing competitions, which is something to think about. As you improve, you are likely to venture further afield, seeking out more successful clubs and higher-calibre coaches. You will also travel longer distances (and more frequently) to competitions.

The rules of fencing set out a framework for the sport. Any attempt to describe a 'best way' of fencing effectively within these rules must be described as a 'theory'. (Manley, 1979) There is a theory, for example, that it requires 10,000 hours of 'deliberate practice' to become an expert in a given field (such as fencing). There are individual differences in how skills are acquired, the learning environment must be correct, which in turn may require a large amount of luck; but it follows that to become world class does indeed take an enormous amount of dedication and practice. (Barraclough, 2013) The best advice from Paul, et al., (2012, p.35) is: 'Don't delay accruing these hours.'

In the final outcome, the extent of your eventual success may be memorable, like this experience recounted by Tim Morehouse:

My opponent slashes hard at my Kevlar jacket and his shout shakes the hall as he takes the first point. Did I even move? I'm the second-to-last US fencer in the team saber competition at the Beijing Olympics. We trail 28–36 in a race to 45. The winner goes on to the gold medal match; the loser fights for the bronze.

I've given twenty years, two-thirds of my life, for the right to stand opposite Russia's Alexsey Yakimenko on this fourteen-metre strip… Yakimenko and I retake our en garde lines, facing each other from twelve feet away with our sword hands raised. I can't see through Yakimenko's mask but I can feel him, confident and ready.

Since the 1960s, Russia has taken almost every Olympic gold medal in this event. The most recent American medal in team saber was bronze in 1948. Cameras flash all around us, but inside the mesh of my mask I'm alone, trying to wring the panic from my breath. This is what I work for, I say to myself, as I always do in that moment of stillness before the point begins.

The referee calls, *'En garde. Prêt? Allez!'* and Yakimenko leaps forward to slash past my guard, his saber edge popping against my jacket as I stand there flat-footed and listless. His speed is stunning but more troubling, Yakimenko has gotten inside my head… Yakimenko and I square off again in the en guard position, facing each other completely still, standing as mirror images… He is the sum of his hours of work, the tournaments he's fought, the lessons he's learned on and off the strip, the people in his life, and the fencers who have come before him, And I am the sum of mine…

Allez! Yells the referee, and I jump forward out of the box…

(Morehouse and Sundem, 2012, pp.xi–xiv)

Tim Morehouse, Jason Rogers, Keeth Smart and James Williams (USA) won the team

INTRODUCTION

Exterior view of the 'Bird's Nest' Stadium at night, Summer Olympics, Beijing, 2008. (Photo: Graham Morrison)

Closing ceremony at the 'Bird's Nest' Stadium, Summer Olympics, Beijing, 2008. The closing ceremony was truly spectacular. A total of 204 National Olympic Committees (NOCs) took part, with 132 Olympic and forty-three world records being broken. Amongst the eighty-seven NOCs in the medal count was war-torn Afghanistan, with its first. In sport you can make friends from around the world but especially so at the Olympic Games. Consider the words of the Tang period poet Du Fu: 'It is almost as hard for friends to meet, as for the morning and evening stars.' (Photo: Graham Morrison)

INTRODUCTION

sabre silver medals. France won the gold, Italy won the bronze. (Olympic Movement, 2008) The closing ceremony took place in the 'Bird's Nest' Stadium.

> Grand fireworks and spectacular choreography brought to a close the Beijing Games Sunday as one of the most remarkable Olympics in recent history were declared at an end. Fireworks across China's capital as a crowd of more than 90,000 at the landmark 'Bird's Nest' Stadium watched the pyrotechnics… (CNN, 2008)

Closing ceremony at the 'Bird's Nest' Stadium, Summer Olympics, Beijing, 2008. (Photo: Graham Morrison)

CHAPTER ONE

FITNESS AND TRAINING

Sports training is all about making the right conditioning (training) choices for a particular sport and marrying them to the specific needs of the athlete and/or team.

(Shepherd, 2006, p.ix)

It used to be said that: 'Training for fencing is best done by fencing.' (Hett, 1951, p.118) The implication being that no other form of training was required. However, these days it is considered that fencing requires: 'A base

Camden International Cadet Sabre girls' individual semi-final, London, 2014. Japan's Misaki Emura, left, fights Lucia Lucarini of Italy. Emura went on to win gold in the final by beating Caroline Queroli of France 15/14. Both these fights were close with some drama, especially in this semi-final when the Korean coach of the Japanese squad produced a 'coach's intervention' to no avail. (Photo: Graham Morrison)

FITNESS AND TRAINING

Camden International Cadet Sabre girls' individual final, London, 2014. Misaki Emura of Japan, left, fights Caroline Queroli of France. Emura won 15/14. (Photo: Graham Morrison)

for fitness and flexibility gained through a well-balanced regime of diet and exercise is essential to any aspiring fencer.' (Kingston, 2001, p.62) This is because modern fencing is a dynamic sport and most training is done at speed, with the greatest physical demands being placed on the legs. (Pitman, 1988)

'Fencing is classed as an "intermittent high-intensity sport", as there are periods of very high intensity along with periods of low inten-

FITNESS AND TRAINING

sity and quite a lot of rest in between bouts. The duration of an international fencing competition can be between nine to eleven hours, however, of that time only 18 per cent will be actual fencing.' (Paul, et al., 2012, p.7)

But: 'The longer you are competing in a fencing competition the more tired you are likely to become as the recovery time becomes less effective.' (Paul, et al., 2012, p.35) Fitness is a necessary precondition for handling the workload requirements of training, and for sustained high performance at fencing tournaments, where a fencer is required to be quick, explosive and persistent. (Barth and Beck, 2007) Consequently, concentration and self-confidence tend to be greater among fitter fencers who are less fatigued. (Wojciechowski, n.d.) These days, it is generally understood that physical fitness is of interest to us all, since it affects our everyday quality of life. The amount of energy we expend in a day will affect our mental states, attitudes and moods. (Shaff, 1982)

The photographs that feature later in this chapter show fencers of various standards juxtaposed in poules. Despite the competitive element, there is a lot of good natured rivalry going on. Friends and family watch from the sidelines, occasionally getting caught up in the drama. If you have never been to a fencing competition like this, try visiting one after the action has started and blend in with the crowd.

Being physically fit enough to fence at a high level is undoubtedly a contributing factor towards success and requires appropriate training choices.

Physical Fitness

The term 'physical fitness' generally refers to the overall physical fitness of an individual, but a number of components contribute to the whole:

- Endurance – the capacity to continue prolonged physical activity of low intensity, despite the onset of fatigue.
- Flexibility – the range of movement at a joint or a series of joints.
- Strength – the maximum force which a muscle group, or group of muscles, can generate against a resistance.
- Speed – the time taken to coordinate the movement of individual joints or of the body as a whole.

(Hazeldine and Cadman, 1984)

Lack of endurance can result in injury. Tired athletes will attempt to make moves that are beyond their physical capacity, resulting in damage to muscles. Fatigue also has a disastrous effect on coordination. (Brown and Adamson, 1995) Fitness and flexibility are also essential to fencing success and both are preventative measures against injury. (Paul, et al., 2012)

> The golden rules for avoiding injury are:
>
> - Be fit for your sport.
> - Check your kit and equipment for wear and tear.
> - Check the competition and training environment for hazards.
> - Always warm up and cool down.
> - Allow your body to adapt to higher levels of training.
>
> (Brown and Adamson, 1995, p.36)

Speed is important in modern fencing. Prof. Zbigniew Czajkowski (cited in SSTT, 2011, p.116) says: 'Fencing is, par excellence, a fast

15

FITNESS AND TRAINING

Sabreurs and épéeists participate in the early rounds of the M8 Open, Bathgate, 2013.

FITNESS AND TRAINING

sport, in every sense of the word (speed of perception, speed of reaction, speed of movement, fast change of action, change of rhythm, etc...' One of the best ways of improving a fencer's performance is to engage in lots of practice bouts. It follows, therefore, that to increase (effective) fencing speed, a fencer should repeatedly practise fast fencing bouts. (Bandrei, 2012)

Speed is inherent and no amount of training will improve its given level by more than about 10 per cent. Running speed can improve significantly more than 10 per cent, because, although it is affected by inherent speed, it is also affected by the range and strength of movement. But intrinsic speed (on its own) is a quality that you have from birth and relates only to physiological parameters, such as the type of muscle you are born with. Strength, on the other hand, can be increased by a factor of approximately 400 per cent. (Winch, 2004) Many people can compensate for a deficiency in speed with a heightened sense of tempo, a steady point, good nerves, patience, etc. (Lukovich, 2013)

The human skeleton is covered in about 600 muscles, which account for about 40 per cent of the body's weight. Muscles are a collection of long fibres made up of cells and grouped into bundles, which are wrapped in a sheath that protects and hold them together. They are organized in pairs. Each muscle has a partner that produces the opposite effect; when one muscle tenses, the other contracts. These muscle partners are controlled by the brain and nervous system. The heart, lungs and blood vessels act as the body's supply system. They supply the muscles with the necessary fuels – oxygen, water and building materials (protein) – and carry away waste products such as lactic acid, heat and carbon dioxide. (Hazeldine and Cadman, 1984) Some muscles are large and some small. They may be close to the surface and just under the skin, or deep inside the body. Their function may be to provide stability or to initiate movement. Muscles have amazing potential for lengthening and shortening. A muscle can shorten 25-30 per cent of resting range when contracted and, when passively stretched, may extend more than 150 per cent of its regular length.

Tendons attach muscles to bone and act to transfer tension to the bones, thereby facilitating movement. Ligaments bind bone to bone, holding the bones in place and thereby supporting the joints. Depending on its structure, a joint can provide either stability or mobility, and those that provide mobility are of most interest to sportspeople. (Brown and Adamson, 1995) 'Strong adequate musculature leads to good balance and balance is the key to mobility in fencing.' (Alaux, 1975, p.183)

Winch (2005, p.14) draws the following distinctions: 'Mobility is the range of movement allowed by the joints. Suppleness is the range of movement allowed by the muscle-tendon soft tissue structures.'

The length of time that an athlete has been doing a particular sport is also relevant. The term 'training maturity' refers to the number of years that an athlete has been training at their sport. If you have trained as a fencer since childhood, you are likely to be more mature, in this sense, than an adult who has recently started. (Shepherd, 2006)

Training maturity will influence:

- the type and intensity of training that the athlete can handle;
- the athlete's bank of appropriate skills (and their ability to pick up new ones);
- the physiological responsiveness of the athlete's body;
- the athlete's mental readiness, motivation and focus.

(Shepherd, 2006, p.15)

FITNESS AND TRAINING

Foilists participate in the early rounds of the M8 Open, Bathgate, 2013.

Warm-Up

During a competition the fencers shown in these photographs are likely to warm up several times, to a greater or lesser degree, even if only by bouting with a friend. Czajkowski (2005, p.365) mentions that 'In the direct elimination rounds, it is often necessary to perform an additional, short warm-up before each bout – especially if the intervals between them are prolonged. Such a warm-up may consist of a few limbering and flexibility exercises, and a few fast movements of weapons, accompanied by a lunge or flèche.'

During physical training or competition, the body has to work hard to adapt to higher levels of stress. That is why it is necessary to warm up first in preparation for the increased energy demands that will be imposed. There are three main reasons for doing this:

- To protect against injury by raising deep muscle temperature and by stretching the muscles, ligaments and connective tissues. This raised temperature will also slightly increase the speed of contraction and the force exerted by the muscle, while reducing viscous resistance in the muscle.
- To improve the body's efficiency by raising the heart, metabolic and respiratory rates.
- To practise and improve performance. Although it cannot be said that a warm-up improves skill, it can assist good performance.

(Hazeldine and Cadman, 1984)

The body works more efficiently when warm. A warm-up allows the body tissues to work more efficiently. While relaxed, the muscles receive only about 15 per cent of the total amount of blood; the rest goes to body organs such as the brain, liver and intestines. During vigorous exercise, the muscles need far more fuel to provide energy and their requirement for blood increases to 80 per cent of the total blood flow, which needs some time to adjust before the muscles can work efficiently. For this reason, it is inadvisable to exercise too soon after eating a heavy meal because the blood needs to remain around the stomach and intestines to absorb the digested food. Exercising too soon will move the blood away from the digestive organs and into the working muscles.

The extent of exercise required for an effective warm-up will depend on the individual's fitness level. Changes in body temperature vary with body size, fat level and rate of body metabolism. To be effective, the warm-up should be intensive enough to cause mild sweating. When this happens, the inside (core) temperature of the body has increased by about one degree Centigrade. As we are trying to raise body temperature, it is preferable to wear warm clothing to retain body heat. Warm-up activities should be continuous and rhythmic in nature and should last ten to fifteen minutes. (Norris, 1994)

It has been suggested (Lukovich, 1998, p.15) that on occasions warming up with a fencing lesson at major competitions may be undertaken for psychological purposes. On the one hand, this mobilizes physical performance and, on the other, it can reduce factors that can have a detrimental effect on performance.

Proprioception is the ability of the brain to sense the position of a joint or how the body is positioned. Evidence from recent research demonstrates that proprioceptive training programmes are effective in improving dynamic balance in footballers and in reducing the rate of ankle sprain in athletes. (Roberts, 2011 cited in Esteves, et al., 2015, p.19)

The following exercise can be practised regularly as part of a warm-up routine:

Stand on one foot on a flat surface with relaxed, upright posture and with your opposite leg bent at the knee; keep your eyes open and maintain this position for 30 seconds before changing sides. Next, repeat the exercise for 30 seconds with your eyes closed. To make the exercise harder, stand on one foot on a soft surface (such as a pillow) for 30 seconds with your eyes closed. Make sure that you have something available to grab if you lose your balance. (Esteves, et al., 2015)

Stretching and Flexibility

Wojciechowski observes that: 'Stretching concerns muscles and flexibility concerns joints, ligaments, tendons and muscles surrounding the joints.' After stretching, the muscles will only remain elongated for a few hours, so ideally a stretching session should build into your daily routine.' (Gunnell, 2001) Flexibility is governed by individual bone structure and soft tissue. Good flexibility allows the muscles to move efficiently through their range, allowing optimal performance with relatively little chance of injury. (Garret, Kaidanov and Pezza, 1995) This enables the fencer to move as required, in any given situations, without undue strain on ligaments, or muscles and tendons. (Bower, 1997) Lack of flexibility is a frequent cause of poor performance and poor technique. Poor flexibility can also hinder speed and endurance. (Hazeldine and Cadman, 1984)

The most important external factor affecting flexibility is temperature. When warmed, body tissues become more pliable. A thorough warm-up should therefore be performed before full-range stretching exercises are

FITNESS AND TRAINING

attempted. (Norris, 1994) 'By increasing the possible range of movement in the shoulder, hips, trunk and ankles, it is possible to improve both speed and agility, as well as to save energy. This in turn means that the performer can play harder and longer. But remember that the amount of stretch achieved will not be of benefit unless it is accompanied by an increase in muscle strength.' (Hazeldine and Cadman, 1984, p.22)

Stretching is easy to learn. To begin, spend ten to thirty seconds in an 'easy stretch'. Go to the point where you feel a mild tension and relax as you hold the stretch. The feeling of tension should then subside. The 'easy stretch' reduces muscular tightness and prepares the tissues for the 'developmental stretch'. To perform the 'developmental stretch', move a fraction of an inch further until you again feel a mild tension and hold for ten to thirty seconds. The 'developmental stretch' fine-tunes the muscles and increases flexibility. Ensure that you breathe slowly, rhythmically and under control. If bending forward to do a stretch, exhale as you bend, and then breathe slowly as you hold the stretch. Avoid holding your breath while stretching. (Anderson, 1981) The target muscles should be as relaxed as possible prior to moving into the stretch position. With minimum tension in the muscle, this should ensure that when the individual moves slowly into the stretch position the connective tissue is able to stretch more effectively. (Brown and Adamson, 1995)

There are many different types of stretching exercises to choose from. The following will help you get started. Each stretch should last between ten and thirty seconds, depending on which textbook you read. Take your time and start with brief stretches until you find your personal comfort zone (if in doubt seek professional advice). Brown and Adamson (1995, p.25) have shown that recommen-

GUIDELINES FOR STRETCHING

- Make sure you are relaxed fully before starting your stretching routine.
- Don't begin stretching until the muscles are warmed up.
- Ease into the stretch to the point where it is comfortable; it should never be painful. Never strain, because this may damage the muscles.
- Stretch so that the pull is felt in the bulky central portion of the muscle. It may be helpful to concentrate on relaxing the muscle or muscle group that is being stretched. Excess tension in the joints can often be relieved by slightly shifting your arms and legs.
- As the feeling of stretching decreases, you should stretch a little further, making sure it still feels comfortable.
- Do not bounce in the end position because of the strain on the muscles being stretched.
- Do not hold your breath: try to breathe calmly and rhythmically to help you relax.
- Concentrate on stretching the weight-bearing muscles in the lower back, hips, knees and ankle.
- Stretch both *before* and *after* each workout. This is the minimum requirement. Stretching after a workout should be particularly encouraged because, not only does it help you to relax and recover, but also the muscles are very warm, and hence easier to relax.

(Hazeldine and Cadman, 1984, pp.24–25)

FITNESS AND TRAINING

dations from researchers and practitioners can vary considerably.

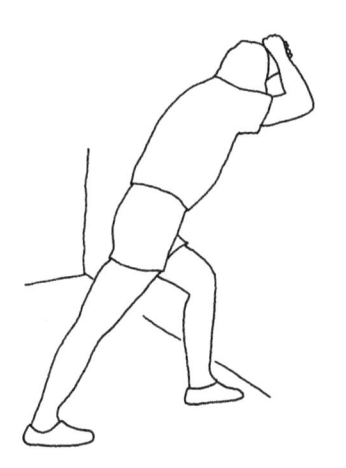

To stretch your calf muscle, stand a little away from a wall. (Anderson, 1981, p.71)

To stretch the calf muscle, stand a little away from a wall, leaning on it with your forearms, head resting on your hands. Bend one leg and place your foot on the ground in front, with the other leg straight behind. Slowly move the hips forward, keeping the lower back flat. Keep the heel of the straight leg on the floor, with toes pointed straight ahead or slightly turned in as you hold the stretch. Now stretch the other leg. (Anderson, 1981)

To stretch the calf muscle and Achilles tendon, lower the hip as you slightly bend the knee of the previously straight leg, keeping the back flat. The back foot should be slightly toed-in or straight ahead during the stretch, with the heel down. This is a useful stretch for developing ankle flexibility. The Achilles tendon area requires only a slight feeling of stretch. (Anderson, 1981)

To stretch the outside of the hip, begin as for the calf stretch. Slightly rotate the hip of the straightened rear leg outwards. (Anderson, 1981, p.71)

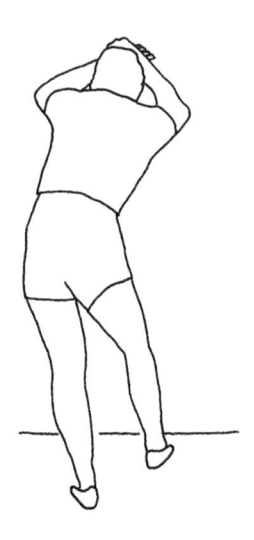

To stretch the outside of the hip, begin as for the previous exercise. Stretch the right side of your hip by slightly turning the right hip to the inside. At the same time, lean the shoulders in the opposite direction to the hips. Hold and stretch, then do the other side. The foot of the back leg should point straight ahead with the heel flat on the ground. (Anderson, 1981)

To stretch the calf muscle and Achilles tendon, begin as before but lower your hips. (Anderson, 1981, p.71)

21

FITNESS AND TRAINING

To stretch your arms and shoulders, sit, or stand with your legs apart and arms overhead. Hold the elbow of one arm with the hand of the other. (ACSM, 2003, p.118)

Gently pull the elbow behind your head, keeping the back and neck in alignment as you stretch. (ACSM, 2003, p.118)

Stand or sit upright with arm and shoulder fully flexed, the elbow pointing towards the ceiling and the palm of the hand placed flat against the back. Grasp the raised elbow with the opposite hand and gently pull the elbow behind the head. Slowly lean the torso with the pull of the elbow until you feel the stretch on the other side of the back. Hold this stretch and relax, then repeat on the opposite side. (Brown and Adamson, 1995)

Sit or stand with your legs apart and arms overhead. Hold the elbow of one arm with the hand of the other. Gently pull the elbow behind the head. (Hazeldine, 1985) Hold this stretch and relax, then switch sides.

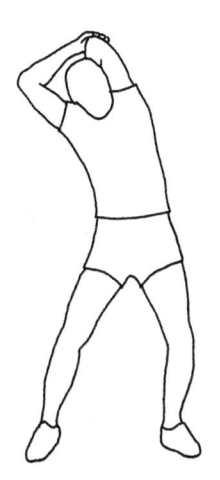

Next, slowly lean the torso with the pull of the elbow until you feel the stretch on the other side of the back. (Brown and Adamson, 1995, p.70)

Start in a standing position with feet turned out, shoulder-width apart. Place one hand on the outside of the thigh and extend the opposite arm above the head. (Brown and Adamson, 1995, p.77)

Begin standing upright with feet turned out, shoulder-width apart. Bend the knees, keeping the feet flat on the floor, the back upright with the pelvis centred. Place one hand on the outside of the thigh and extend the opposite arm above the head, leaning as far as is comfortable in the direction of the hand on the thigh. Hold this stretch and relax, then change sides. Remember to breathe in the stretch position. If you find this too difficult, this stretch can also be performed with both arms by your sides. (Brown and Adamson, 1995)

FITNESS AND TRAINING

Stand up straight supported by one hand against a wall. Bend one leg at the knee, holding on to the top of the foot with the opposite hand. (Anderson, 1981, p.74)

Hold the top of your foot with the opposite hand and gently put the heel towards the buttocks. Done this way the knee bends at a natural angle. Hold and stretch, then do the other side. (Anderson, 1981)

The next stretching exercise is meant to be performed on a step. Move one foot back until your instep is level with the edge of the step. (Brown and Adamson, 1995, p.98)

The next stretching exercise is meant to be performed on a step. Begin by standing upright on the step, with feet parallel, about hip-width apart. You may hold on to a handrail if you wish. Move one foot back until your instep is level with the edge of the step. Keep your body weight forward while pressing the heel downward. Hold this stretch and relax, then stretch with the other leg. (Brown and Adamson, 1995)

Stand upright with the feet a normal walking pace apart. Rotate one foot, so that the feet are now at right angles. Lunge until the knee is over the instep of the leading foot. (Brown and Adamson, 1995, p.92)

This type of exercise is often done in fencing clubs. Stand upright, with the feet a normal walking pace apart. Rotate one foot, so that the feet are now at right angles (akin to an on guard position). Lunge as a fencer, until the knee is over the instep of the leading shoe. Hold this stretch and relax. Then rotate both feet, adopting a lunge position in the opposite direction, and stretch again.

The lunge is the beginning of the athlete's training in the lunging motion. When done correctly, the lunge helps to build strength in the legs and back and contributes to safety, efficiency and power. (James, 2006)

23

FITNESS AND TRAINING

Stand upright with the feet a normal walking pace apart. Move one foot forward, with the knee positioned directly over the ankle and the other knee touching the floor behind. (Hazeldine, 1985, p.59)

Move one foot forward until the knee is directly over the ankle and the rear knee is touching the floor behind, the rear leg extended. Lower the hips, keeping them square to the front and using the hands for balance on either side. Ensure that both feet are in line and not turned out. Hold this stretch, and then do the other side. To increase this stretch, straighten the rear leg and gently lean the trunk up and back. Push with the arms by placing the hands on the bent knee. (Hazeldine, 1985)

Sit on the floor with your back upright. Turn your legs out from the hips, bending the knees and pulling the soles of your feet together. (Brown and Adamson, 1995, p.93)

Sit on the floor with back upright. Turn the legs out from the hips, bending the knees and pulling the soles of your feet together towards the buttocks. Place hands just below the ankles, with elbows on the knees. Gently press the legs down towards the floor. (Brown and Adamson, 1995)

Sit on the floor with legs spread out as wide as they will go, knees locked. Slowly bend forward from the hips. (Hazeldine, 1985, p.57)

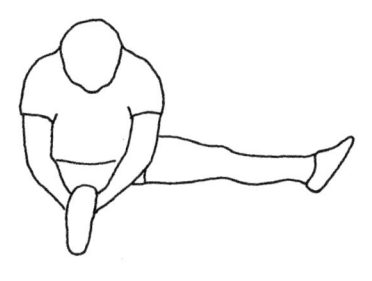

Next, turn to face one of your feet and bend forward, attempting to grasp the ankle. (Hazeldine, 1985, p.57)

Sit on the floor with legs spread out as wide as they will go, knees locked. Slowly bend forward from the hips, ensuring that the top of the thighs remain relaxed. Try to keep your hips from rolling backward and put your hands out in front for support. Hold this stretch and relax. Next, turn to face one of your feet and bend forward, attempting to grasp the ankle. Hold this stretch and relax, then repeat with the other leg. This exercise will also stretch the muscles of the outer shoulders and chest. (Hazeldine and Cadman, 1984)

FITNESS AND TRAINING

Sit on the floor with legs outstretched. Rotate one of your ankles through a complete range of motion. (Hazeldine, 1985, p.58)

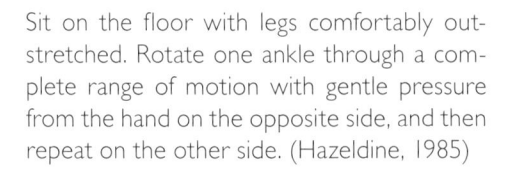

If you find this too difficult, try hooking a towel around your foot. (Hazeldine, 1985, p.57)

Sit on the floor with legs comfortably outstretched. Rotate one ankle through a complete range of motion with gentle pressure from the hand on the opposite side, and then repeat on the other side. (Hazeldine, 1985)

Sit on the floor with one leg outstretched and the sole of the foot on the other touching the inside of the thigh. With head up and back straight, reach down towards the toes on the extended foot. An extra stretch can be attained by pointing the toes back towards the head, or by grasping the ankle and pulling the chest down towards the knee. If you find this too difficult, try hooking a towel around your foot. (Hazeldine, 1985)

Sit on the floor with one leg outstretched and the sole of the foot on the other touching the inside thigh. (Hazeldine, 1985, p.57)

Sit on the floor with one leg outstretched, bending the other, lifting the heel towards the buttocks. (Hazeldine, 1985, p.59)

LEFT: With head up and back straight, reach down towards the toes on the extended foot. (Hazeldine, 1985, p.57)

FITNESS AND TRAINING

Next, tighten the buttocks on the side of the bent leg as the hip is turned up and over. (Hazeldine, 1985, p.59)

Return to the start position and bend forward from the hips over the extended leg, reaching for the ankle. (Hazeldine, 1985, p.59)

Sit on the floor with one leg outstretched, bending the other and pulling the heel towards the buttocks. The foot and knee of the bent leg should touch the floor, with the arms supporting from behind. Gently lean straight back until an easy stretch is felt, keeping the knee of the bent leg on the floor. Hold this stretch and relax. Next, tighten the buttocks on the side of the bent leg as the hip is turned up and over. Hold this stretch and relax. Still with the right leg bent, return to the start position and bend forward from the hips over the extended leg. Reach for the ankle and use the arm muscles to pull the body down, keeping the head up. Take particular care if prone to knee problems. (Hazeldine, 1985)

Warm-Down

In a competition environment, fencers will alternate between heightened states of activity and moments of comparative relaxation. In the photographs that follow, fencers are seen observing their opponents while waiting to be called to fence or gathering around the poule sheet at the conclusion of a round to study the final results.

Other competition photographs also appear at the end of this chapter.

During intense exercise the beating of the heart is helped by the contraction of the exercising limb muscles. As these muscles contract, they squeeze the blood vessels that travel through them, thus helping the blood to return to the heart. If an athlete stops exercising abruptly, the limb muscles no longer pump the blood vessels and help the heart. The demand placed on the heart increases and the pulse will actually get faster although exercise has stopped. (Norris, 1994)

Returning the body to a more steady state after a workout will promote recovery and reduce subsequent injury. Most warm-downs will utilize a period of easy cardiovascular activity and gentle stretches. (Shepherd, 2006) The body must make a number of adaptations during the recovery period before it can return to normal. This does not happen immediately. The muscles that have been pumping the blood back to the heart are no longer active, which results in a build-up of excess fluid in the muscle. The muscle forces are not sufficient to move the blood out of the muscle, and this may cause stiffness or soreness in the muscle, or possibly muscle cramps. Stiffness may be avoided by continuing to move the affected muscles in a gentle, rhythmic manner, until the body returns to a near resting state. (Hazeldine and Cadman, 1984) Brown and

FITNESS AND TRAINING

Waiting between rounds at the M8 Open, Bathgate, 2013.

Observing the opposition while waiting to be called at the M8 Open, Bathgate, 2013. (1)

Observing the opposition while waiting to be called at the M8 Open, Bathgate, 2013. (2)

27

FITNESS AND TRAINING

Observing the opposition while waiting to be called at the M8 Open, Bathgate, 2013. (3)

Checking results at the end of a round at the M8 Open, Bathgate, 2013.

Adamson (1995, p.37) suggest: 'The most effective cool down is five to ten minutes of aerobic exercise on a stationary bike, rowing machine, or jogging machine at an intensity that enables you to talk without being out of breath.'

Blood is still needed in the muscles after exercise in order to aid recovery, so you should not eat a large meal immediately. If you feel hungry, you can eat a small amount of sweet, high-carbohydrate food such as a banana or a piece of toast with honey. Following training, time must be allowed for the body to change and adapt. Rest for recovery from exercise is vital. (Norris, 1994) Morgan (2007, p.94) notes: 'There are several things

FITNESS AND TRAINING

that will tell you when you are not getting enough recovery time:

- Elevated pulse in the morning.
- General feeling of tiredness.
- Sore throat.
- Your legs will feel heavy.
- You may experience a lack of enthusiasm.
- Your progress will come to a standstill, or you may even see a regression in results.

A number of changes happen when the body works particularly hard, which is what we will consider next.

Overload

In order to develop strength you must make the muscles work with slightly more load on them than they can manipulate comfortably. This type of work is characteristically slow and sustained. The two methods of overloading muscle against resistance are isometric and isotonic exercises.

Isometric exercise is the contraction of the muscle against a force that is so great that it does not change its length, or shorten. The act of pushing your right hand against your left hand so that neither hand moves is an isometric exercise. Isotonic exercise occurs when a muscle contracts to a different length. To increase strength, isotonic exercise must occur with resistance, as moving your limb while holding a weight through a range of motion of your joint. When you have completed a knee bend you have exercised isotonically. Your thigh and leg muscles have moved, while supporting the weight of your body through the range of motion of your hip, knee and ankle joints. If you lift a dumbbell through a range of motion, you are also isotonically exercising. If you stop the dumbbell halfway through and hold it motionless, you are isometrically exercising. (Wyrick, 1971)

Hazeldine and Cadman (1984, p.12) suggest: 'The principle of overload is based on three factors:

- Frequency: the number of sessions per week, per month, per year.
- Intensity: the training loads per week, per month, per year.
- Time: the duration of training in hours per week, per month, per year.'

Unless the body is subjected to a certain stress level, its condition is unlikely to improve. Below this level you will only maintain the current level of fitness. A number of changes occur when overload occurs: the nervous system encourages the formation of more muscle fibre, the circulatory system learns to distribute more blood to the muscles that need it, and the overload stimulates the muscular system to produce extra protein to help meet the extra demands which the body anticipates. (Hazeldine and Cadman, 1984) As fitness improves, exercise must get harder so the body continues to be taxed. The body has adapted to the training load, so further improvement will only occur if the training intensity is increased. If training for stamina, the intensity of exercise is indicated by the pulse rate; if training for strength, intensity may be measured by the weight lifted; and when training for flexibility the range of movement and length of time a stretch can be held is an indication of intensity. (Norris, 1994)

In weight training, overload is done by selecting weights that are heavy enough to cause the muscles to work at their maximum capacity, and then progressively increasing the weight until the muscles become stronger. (Hazeldine and Cadman, 1984)

James (2006, p.27) advises that 'The most basic plan is to work one overload session a week. Between overloading sessions, the athlete should work easier sessions where the body is not overloaded and has a chance to recover. *This principle applies to all training sessions*, whether they are predominantly skill oriented, strength oriented, or a mixture of the two… Posture and exercise form should be excellent every day, not just on one overload day per week. Good exercise form and posture must be learned just like any other skill. Once the athlete can execute each exercise with good form and posture, *the loss of good form becomes the measure of fatigue*. Form and posture should be perfect and automatic. Cease repetitions of the exercise when your form fails, rest, and then, if necessary, do another set *with good form*.'

A number of guidelines are shown in the panel Overload in Weight Training.

A set is a term used for a group of repetitions. For strength gain, sets are performed consecutively, not one set of one exercise followed by one set of another. The reason for this is that the muscle groups get progressively more tired and more effort must be applied to perform the exercise. This is called stage training. In a circuit, the exercise is performed only once every cycle, and thus there is more time to recover than in stage training. (Winch, 2004) 'Circuit training is a method of physical training that employs both conditioning exercises and weight training. It has proved an effective means of increasing not only muscular endurance but also strength. It has also been shown to produce positive changes in motor performance, general fitness, muscular power, endurance and speed.' (Hazeldine and Cadman, 1984, p.57)

Effects of Training

Overloading creates a training effect; however, if training stops, these benefits will be lost. (Norris, 1994) Endurance can be lost in a third of the time it takes to achieve it. Strength, on the other hand, declines more slowly. Long period of inactivity should be avoided. (Hazeldine and Cadman, 1984)

Norris (1994, p.46) suggests: 'In just twenty days of total rest, stamina reduces by 25 per cent – a loss of about 1 per cent per day. Strength reduction is even greater, with average losses over the same period of 35 per cent. Muscles that have become more flexible with training will slowly tighten again, and muscle imbalance may occur if some muscles tighten more quickly than others. Skill-based components including sports technique, balance and coordination last longer, but will gradually degrade with time… The immediate effects are the body's response to exercise. These are brought about by increased metabolism and include higher heart and breathing rates, changes in blood flow, increased body temperature, and chemical alterations to enzymes within the working muscles. When exercise stops, the body tries to reduce its metabolic rate to resting level once more and the short-term training effects due to recovery become apparent. Body temperature has increased, so sweating continues to try to cool the tissues. Energy has been used and must be replaced, so breathing rate and heart rate remain high. Waste products have been formed as energy was "burnt", and these wastes must be eliminated.'

Rate of Perceived Exertion

When exercising regularly, it is helpful to have a 'rule of thumb' that suggests how hard you are exerting yourself. One of the most effective ways of keeping track of the intensity is to monitor how hard a workout feels. To work out your personal intensity levels, use the

FITNESS AND TRAINING

OVERLOAD IN WEIGHT TRAINING (ABRIDGED)

1. Loading
The best exercise load for general training is a weight that you can raise ten times in succession. You should continue to work with this load until you can manage *fifteen* repetitions, at which point you should increase the weight so as to reduce the number of possible repetitions to ten again.

However, if you are using weights *for the very first time*, you should start with a (lighter) load which you can lift *correctly* for fifteen repetitions. This weight will differ for each exercise, depending on the strength of the muscles. Only after only two or three sessions should you change to a weight that you can properly handle for only ten repetitions…

2. Frequency
On average, you should do weight training two or three times a week. Each session should last from thirty minutes to an hour. The duration will, of course, depend on your physical condition and the speed at which you exercise. One session normally consists of three sets of each exercise…

3. Speed
The optimum speed of repetition will vary, depending on the muscle group used. If the movement is speeded up, the exercise will become shorter and less effective as a strength builder…

4. Rest
- Rest between repetitions should be kept to a minimum, ideally normally less than one second, depending on your use of the rebound at the end of each movement, which initiates the next movement.
- The rest interval between sets should be between one and two minutes, depending on how intense the next set is going to be.
- After a session of heavy lifting using a particular muscle group, you should rest for at least forty-eight hours: the exact period may vary depending on your physical condition.
- If you work on chest and legs on Monday and Thursday, and back, shoulders and arms on Tuesday and Friday, this will give at least seventy-two hours for each muscle group to recover. This system is known as a *split routine*.

5. Specificity
Choose exercises that are applicable to the requirements of your particular sport – ones that are as similar as possible in their movement pattern, speed of movement and muscle contraction…

(Hazeldine and Cadman, 1984, pp.46–47)

FITNESS AND TRAINING

Monitoring Your Rate of Perceived Exertion (abridged)

Perceived Exertion	How Hard Does It Feel?	Breathing	Per Cent Aerobic Capacity
1	Resting	Normal	35
2	Minimal activity such as sitting at a desk working	Normal	45
3	Gentle activity – you begin to feel slightly warmer	Comfortable	55
4	Your heart rate is starting to rise and you're feeling slightly warmer. Sustainable, but definitely exercise	Deeper but regular	65
5	Quite hard. You're starting to sweat	Deep but still steady	75
6	Between hard and very hard	Getting heavier	85
7	Very hard. You're sweating hard and feeling hot	Deep and fast	90
8	Strenuous	Very fast and deep	95
9–10	The absolute hardest effort you can possibly make – you couldn't go any faster. Your muscles are burning	Your breathing becomes laboured. You have now passed the 'anaerobic threshold'	96–100

(Waterson, 2003, p.99)

rate of perceived exertion. (Waterson, 2003) This is shown in the Panel entitled Monitoring Your Rate of Perceived Exertion. In this, 'aerobic capacity' is the maximum rate at which oxygen can be consumed per minute. (Friedberg, 1984)

The difference between the aerobic and anaerobic energy systems can be explained as follows: 'The aerobic energy system uses oxygen, and burns carbohydrate, fats and proteins. It is relatively slow at producing energy, and therefore cannot be used when a lot of energy is needed quickly...For more intense activity, the body uses anaerobic energy systems, which don't require oxygen but which rapidly result in waste products... that build up in the muscles and use up limited stores of glycogen...The *aerobic threshold* is the level of effort at which anaerobic energy pathways start to be a significant part of energy production. Runners want to increase their aerobic threshold because this will enable them to run faster for longer before they tip into anaerobic metabolism, which cannot be sustained for long...The *anaerobic threshold* is defined as the level of exercise intensity at which lactic acid builds up in the body faster than it can be cleared away.' (Barder, 2002, pp.104–105)

Each person experiences exertion in their own way. For some, level 9 may be reached quickly, yet others may be content to exercise at much lower rates of perceived exertion. After an aerobic capacity of 85 per cent (level 6), holding a conversation is likely to be difficult; and after 90 per cent (level 7), conversation is likely to be extremely limited. (Waterson, 2003)

FITNESS AND TRAINING

Main Points

- Overall physical fitness requires endurance, flexibility, strength and speed. Although a fencer's inherent speed cannot be increased significantly, strength can.
- Warm-up activities tend to be continuous, rhythmic and last ten to fifteen minutes. When warm, the body becomes more pliable; this is why stretching exercises are performed after the warm-up. The 'easy stretch' reduces muscular tightness and prepares the tissues for the 'developmental stretch', which fine-tunes the muscles and increases flexibility.
- Warm-down activities return the body to a relatively steady state after exercise and last ten to fifteen minutes.
- With isometric exercise, a muscle does not change its length, or shorten. Isotonic exercise occurs when a muscle contracts to a different length.
- Overload is caused by the frequency of training, intensity of loads and the duration of training activities.
- For stamina, intensity of training is shown by pulse rate; for strength, intensity is measured by the weight lifted; and for flexibility, the range of movement or amount of time a stretch may be held is a measure of this type of intensity.
- To hold on to the effects of training it is necessary to use them.

Leon Paul Cup men's individual foil semi-final, London, 2013. Great Britain's Kristjan Archer, left, takes on Maor Hatoel of Israel. Hatoel won 15/7. (Photo: Graham Morrison)

FITNESS AND TRAINING

ABOVE: Leon Paul Cup men's individual foil final, London, 2013. Italy's Tobia Biondo, left, fights Maor Hatoel of Israel. The fight was close with the early advantage to the Italian. Hatoel caught and passed him for 7/6. From here, they traded hits with Biondo leading just once more for 12/11, after which Hatoel took charge. (Photo: Graham Morrison)

LEFT: Leon Paul Cup men's individual foil final, London, 2013. Tobia Biondo of Italy, left, takes on Israel's Maor Hatoel. (Photo: Graham Morrison)

CHAPTER TWO

STRENGTH AND CONDITIONING

Good strength training creates not just muscle but smart muscle.
>(James, 2006, p.159)

'Conditioning' is the most important word in the athlete's vocabulary: it is the essence of athletic performance and survival in the heat of competition and, without it, athletic lives are short and never reach the heights promised by their potential.
>(Winch, 2005, p.9)

Introduction

The character of a team fencing tournament is quite different to that of a competition. In the photographs that follow, male and female teams fence foil, sabre and épée, (a total of six weapons).

The fencers warm up prior to each team match, which accounts for some of them wearing tracksuit bottoms while fencing to retain warmth. Occasionally, one of the coaches will step forward with a warm-up

Fencers, coaches and officials congregate at the Five Nations Tournament, Edinburgh, 2013. (2)

Épée warm-up at the Five Nations Tournament, Edinburgh, 2013.

35

STRENGTH AND CONDITIONING

Sabre warm-up at the Five Nations Tournament, Edinburgh, 2013.

lesson, perhaps to prepare someone psychologically for a crucial encounter. All of these fencers will have trained in order to be at their best and words such as 'strength' and 'conditioning' are now prevalent in fencing circles.

Paul, *et al.* (2012, p.76) suggest that: 'Strength and conditioning training will improve your power and speed, which in turn will improve your fencing. Using weights is a very efficient way of conditioning your body. Even two hours per week, that is, a one-hour session on two separate days, can double the strength of your body in six months, male or female – assuming a start-point where you don't usually do any physical work or other exercise.' However, as James (2006, p.11) points out: 'Fencers are not bodybuilders! They need a workout programme that *begins* with basic weightlifting techniques, then veers away from basic strength exercises into modern, *sports*-oriented exercises.' Leg power is needed for rapid fencing mobility, maintenance of distance, fast attacks carrying the body weight whilst maintaining balance at all times. Leg muscles need to be strong and fast. Weight training (as opposed to weightlifting) is required to develop this kind of muscle. 'Weight training' means exercising with light weights using a high number of repetitions. (Anderson, 1973)

Warm-up lesson at the Five Nations Tournament, Edinburgh, 2013.

STRENGTH AND CONDITIONING

Conditioning

Conditioning is the work needed by the athlete to prepare for the stresses and strains of eventual specific training and competition. Aerobic conditioning improves the ability of the athlete to operate physically for long periods of time and is normally undertaken without an external resistance, moving just the body weight.

The most basic form of aerobic conditioning is any exercise that makes the athlete's pulse and breathing rate increase moderately and sustainably, as during steady running, cycling, rowing and walking. The lower heart rate and the relaxation enable athletes to learn the necessary skills to improve their concentration and mental focus. Aerobic conditioning increases the speed of recovery by improving the body's transport systems via which the breakdown products and unwanted metabolites (by-products of metabolism) are taken to the liver and kidneys for removal from the blood. The efficiency of the cardiovascular system determines to a great extent the aerobic fitness of an individual, which can be improved dramatically by training. Mobility conditioning is needed to ensure each joint has maximum range of movement. Increasing suppleness is also a necessary aspect of regular conditioning. As the muscles and tendons are worked over the years there is a tendency for them to shorten, thus reducing the range of effective movement. Athletes should be encouraged to work on mobility and suppleness as part of their conditioning programmes. (Winch, 2004 and 2005)

Core Stability

Without core stability it is not possible to perform skilfully, or accurately, the more difficult manoeuvres in a fencing bout.

The term 'core stability' is used to focus on the problems relating to obtaining and maintaining correct posture during athletic performance. Good conditioning of the muscles of the spine, sides, abdomen, hips, ankles and other stabilized areas of the body is important if the athlete is to perform correct and balanced movement of the limbs. The muscles that stabilize the core of the body do so by working isometrically; they hold their contractions in fixed positions for considerable lengths of time.

A fencer crouches low, attempting to place the point on the opponent's target.

STRENGTH AND CONDITIONING

A fencer retains his balance while under pressure.

Take the simple press-up, for example. This exercise requires the athlete to hold the body in a horizontal position supported by the hands and feet. Consider what the mid-region muscles must do when the body is lowered and raised; they must fix the body in a straight line. Since no movement in the mid-region is required, the core stability muscles are acting isometrically all the time. (Winch, 2005) 'Basic weight training has a high core stability conditioning element. For example, the simple back squat requires the athlete to fix the body position while the legs are flexed and then straightened. Since the weight is on the shoulders, considerable strain is created along the full length of the back. Because the effort seems to be in working the legs, the effect on the core is often ignored.' (Winch, 2005, p.46)

Some useful core stability exercises follow:

The press-up requires the athlete to hold his/her body in a horizontal position. (Hazeldine, 1985, p.73)

STRENGTH AND CONDITIONING

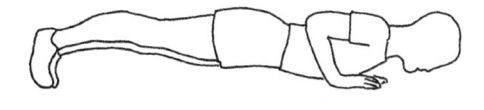

The arms are then bent so the body lowers to the floor. (Hazeldine, 1985, p.73)

For a press-up, begin in the support position with arms shoulder-width apart. Bend the arms to lower the chest to the floor, and then return to the support position. Ensure the body is held rigid throughout. There are a number of variations worth mentioning. Try performing the press-up as before but resting on the fingertips. Press up explosively, touch chest with both hands, then replace the hands on the floor. This version can also be performed by pushing up explosively, clapping the hands and then replacing them on the floor. The press-up may be performed with the feet located on a bench, or one leg may be raised in the air as the arms bend to lower the chest to the floor. You may then repeat with the other leg and keep alternating. (Hazeldine, 1985) Other variations on the press-up include the wide hand position that exercises the pectorals more and the narrow hand position that exercise the triceps. (Winch, 2005)

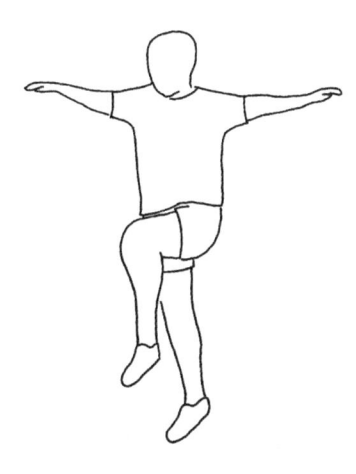

...then balances on one leg, with the knee of the other leg raised, so the top of the thigh is parallel with the ground. (Winch, 2005, pp.41–43)

Also, you can begin with one hand on a foam block. Lower the body until the elbows and shoulders are in line, and then return to the start position. The block is alternated between hands for balanced development. This will exercise the shoulder above the block, which must stabilize when the force comes from a different angle. Another variation is the jump press-up on to two foam blocks. Partially flex the elbows and immediately push up explosively. Move both hands over the blocks and land in the press-up position. Step down one hand at a time to resume the start position. (James, 2006)

The athlete stands with arms held out horizontally or to the sides...

STRENGTH AND CONDITIONING

as for standing on two legs, the lower back not being allowed to curve outwards as the knee is raised. In this position the knee can be rotated outward, as near as to 90 degrees as possible, or rotated inward, up towards the stomach. (Winch, 2005)

In this position the knee can be rotated outwards, as near to 90 degrees as possible. (Winch, 2005, pp.41–43)

The body position is fixed, while the legs must flex, then straighten. (Winch, 2005, p.149)

Or it can be rotated inwards, up towards the stomach. (Winch, 2005, pp.41–43)

The next exercise is the standing knee raise. The athlete stands with arms held out horizontally or to the side; then balances on one leg, with the knee of the other leg raised so the top of the thigh is parallel with the ground. The hips should be held in the same position

In the squat position the feet are under the body, the legs bent to lower the body, while the torso remains relatively erect. (Winch, 2005, p.149)

STRENGTH AND CONDITIONING

Before doing a back squat, try attempting a simple body weight squat with your feet a little wider than shoulder-width and hands at your sides. Keep the shoulders back and the spine neutral. From here, sit with the hips back and bend the knees down. Inhale, then exhale and press back up. Make sure that your weight is back in your heels, that you have proper spinal alignment and that you breathe in time with the motion. The back squat is performed by holding the bar on the back of the shoulders (not the neck) in a comfortable position. The head is held up and the eyes focused on a point in front and level with the eyes. Now proceed as before. (Winch, 2005)

The squat teaches the athlete to combine posture and power. The feet are under the body, the legs bend to lower the body while the torso remains fairly erect. For fencers, this is a good general description of the 'on guard' position. There will be some forward lean from the hips as the athlete goes down but it should not bring the head forward beyond the feet. The squat posture is the foundation of all standing athletic movements. It is not easy to maintain a good posture while squatting under even a small load. Even a lightweight squat will point out the athlete's weaknesses very quickly. (James, 2006)

Winch (2004, p29) notes that many athletes find a simple squatting movement hard to do correctly '…usually due to lack of mobility in the ankles or the length of the Achilles tendon. This is why it is recommended that a period of at least one month is needed to learn the basic movements before any resistance above 10 or 20kg is used. In some instances this should be longer if required, particularly if the athlete has a serious lack of joint mobility or muscle-tendon suppleness… Many such athletes have difficulty in touching their toes, or crouching with head up and heels on the ground. It is strongly advised that, if the athlete has this sort of problem, a period of general mobility and suppling is undertaken before strength training is begun. The problem of a lack of suppleness often occurs in younger athletes, usually as a result of rapid bone growth. Care must be taken in this situation not to put undue stress on the athlete as this can lead to physical damage to the growing area of the bone… The best results are gained by making sure that correct tuition is given from the earliest stage…'

There is a number of core stability conditioning exercises that use the Swiss ball:

The athlete sits firmly on the Swiss ball with the body vertical, legs at 90 degrees. (Winch, 2005, p.47)

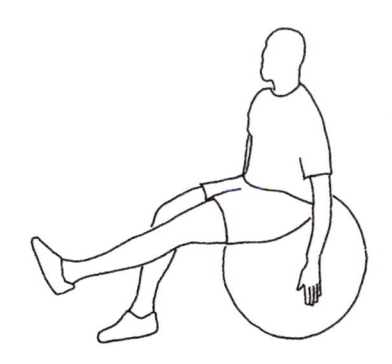

One leg is then raised to the horizontal and held in position. (Winch, 2005, p.47)

41

STRENGTH AND CONDITIONING

The athlete sits firmly on the Swiss ball with the body vertical, legs at 90 degrees. From here, he/she moves slowly forward, until nearly falling off, the feet adjusting so they are once again at 90 degrees. One leg is then raised to the horizontal and held there for the required time, before returning to the start position. The same exercise is then performed with the opposite leg. (Winch, 2005)

degrees. The body must be held very firm and in line with the upper legs. From here, one leg is raised to the horizontal and held there for the required time, before returning to the start position. The same exercise is then performed with the opposite leg. (Winch, 2005)

Start as before. (Winch, 2005, p.48)

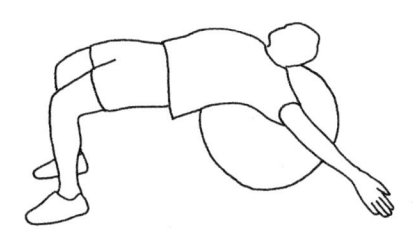

Next, the shoulders lie on the ball, with the body outstretched, held firmly in line with the upper legs. (Winch, 2005, p.47)

This time, push the shoulders to one side, keeping the upper body horizontal. (Winch, 2005, p.48)

One leg is raised to the horizontal and held there. (Winch, 2005, p.47)

Next, the shoulders are rested on the ball with the body outstretched. The arms are held away from the body and legs at 90

Start as before. From here the shoulders are pushed to one side, keeping the upper body horizontal. Once the most extreme position has been attained, it is held for the required

STRENGTH AND CONDITIONING

time before moving to the other side of the ball. (Winch, 2005)

Next, the feet are place on the Swiss ball and a press-up position is adopted with the back straight. (Winch, 2005, p.48)

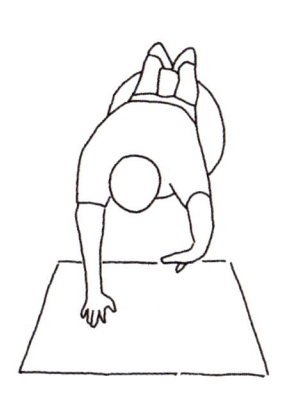

One arm is raised in line with the body. (Winch, 2005, p.48)

For this exercise, the feet are placed on the Swiss ball and a press-up position adopted with the body straight. From here, one arm is raised in line with the body and held there for the required time, before returning it to the floor. Then the other arm is raised. (Winch, 2005)

Strength Training

Strength in fencing is particularly applicable to explosive offensive actions, which cannot be sustained for lengthy periods. (Tau, 2005) James (2006, p.11) advises that he '…cannot guarantee that strength training will make you fence better… if you are healthy, it will make your biomechanical machine function at a higher level. You will feel fitter and stronger. Modern fencing is extremely athletic. You are unlikely to succeed without finely honed physical fitness.' Fencers will maximize their strength potential by developing healthy muscles. Even at maximum effort, 40 per

> **PROGRESS IN STRENGTH DEVELOPMENT DEPENDS UPON…**
>
> - The muscle groups involved: the large muscles allow for quicker improvement because they can withstand greater resistance.
> - The exercise itself: in some exercises the mastery of the skill is the key to greater improvement.
> - The order of work: a fencer may be able to take great resistance on one particular day because he/she is used to working the muscles in a certain order. However, if the work is changed he/she may find he/she is unable to handle the same amount of resistance. For this reason, it is often psychologically better to vary the routine in order to become accustomed to the change.
>
> (Tau, 2005, p.36)

STRENGTH AND CONDITIONING

Core stability is essential when fencing at close quarters. The Five Nations Tournament, Edinburgh, 2013.

STRENGTH AND CONDITIONING

cent of a novice athlete's muscle cells are resting. With training, the athlete may learn to call upon 85 per cent of their muscle mass. (James, 2006)

The panel entitled Progress in Strength Development Depends Upon… lists some factors that may be considered important in strength development in fencing.

James (2006, p.22) points out: 'The muscle is made up of small motor units, each consisting of one nerve supplying a certain number of muscle cells. Each motor unit is either on or off; there is no such thing as halfway on. Some motor units contract when the electrical signal is low, some when it is medium, and some when it is high. The ones that contract with a low impulse will also contract when the nerve signal is medium or high. Some parts of the muscle never contract except in a dire emergency.'

Under the influence of internal and external stimuli, the nervous system enters a state of excitation. During a fencing bout, the fencer has to execute various movements; ideally, each motion should be a conditioned reflex. (Tau, 2005) Fencing requires unusual positions that are not part of the common responses of our physical make-up, and the fencer must 'programme' himself/herself to make the correct moves by reflex. Through constant repetition of precise movements, a fencer trains his/her reflexes to respond to the momentary situation. This is accomplished through lessons and developed through practice. (Alaux, 1975)

A reaction is an action taken in response to certain stimuli. Despite the rapidity of one's reactions, there is an interval of time between the stimulus and the response. This reaction time is determined in part by the time it takes an image formed in the retina to reach the brain, and then for the impulses to activate the muscles of the hand and body. Speed of reaction is directly dependent upon the mobility of the nervous processes of stimulation and inhibition. The more rapidly nerve cells in the central nervous system change over from a state of stimulation to a state of inhibition, the more rapid the reaction. The state of inhibition is not a state of rest; it is an active state of the nerve cells in which stimuli cannot pass through them. The simultaneous processes of stimulation and inhibition are the only thing that permits a living organism to execute various movements. (Tau, 2005)

The nerves become more active and coordinated as the athlete's functional strength increases, even within the first two to three weeks of the programme. However, through disuse, an athlete's nerves become less active, so less muscle mass is stimulated into action. Training optimizes performance by teaching the nervous system to call upon more of the available muscle fibres and call upon all parts of the muscle at the same time. It teaches all the muscles needed to fire at the correct time. It teaches the athlete to recruit the muscle fibres quickly, to send more electrical energy to the muscles. (James, 2006)

James (2006, p.159) refers to this phenomenon as 'smart muscle'. 'Smart muscle can deal with unstable situations… can play its part in the most complicated movement in perfect harmony… knows how to act so that the joints are not damaged.' The body is capable of building new capillaries to supply blood to areas where there is special need for oxygen and nutrients. An athlete cannot express strength without skill and coordination. All the parts within one muscle must learn to contract in unison and all the muscles that make up a large movement must work together. Some move the arm, some stabilize joints and other parts of the body and some decelerate the limb after it moves. In the complete body motion of a fencing lunge, almost every bone, muscle and sinew of the

STRENGTH AND CONDITIONING

body must be in the right place, doing the right job, at the right time. Hence, strength training is a highly skilled task. (James, 2006) Strength training can also bring with it certain psychological benefits. The greatest motivation in fencing is the promise of success and a fencer who believes that strength training contributes significantly to this success will pursue it with dedication and ardour. (Tau, 2005)

For athletic events, movement is produced by the muscles applying force using the bones as levers, the joint being the pivot points. Each joint has a maximum range of movement for the individual concerned. This maximum range of movement is called 'full mobility' of that joint. Normal range only approaches full mobility when there are no restrictions to movement, such as large muscles or injuries. (Winch, 2005) Care must be taken with connective tissue, which takes five to seven times longer to develop than muscle. (James, 2006)

Winch (2004, p.8) suggests: 'We are all conditioned to use the word "strength" as if it had one immutable meaning.' James (2006, pp.19–20) looks at a checklist of parameters of strength for any given sport and considers what is needed for fencing.

- How much force is needed in your sport?
    In fencing, the forces we need to apply are not very great compared to the forces in some other sports.
- How much time do you have to deliver the force needed in your sport?
    Fencers have very little time – often only a fraction of a second – to deliver their hit.
- How often – and for how long – are the forces in your sport required?
    The force required in fencing must be applied over and over again, but only for three minutes followed by a rest period. Maximum effort is applied for periods that rarely reach as much as thirty seconds.
- How much acceleration is required?
    In fencing, extreme acceleration is often necessary – for example, when a lunge or flèche begins from a standing start or when the final movement of an attack must catch a retreating opponent.
- How much deceleration is necessary?
    Fencing requires frequent whole-body deceleration. A fencer must be able to move backward, quickly stop to parry, and go forward quickly to riposte.
    Arm deceleration is also very important in martial arts such as boxing or fencing: the athlete's arm must recover from a missed attempt and prepare for the next action.
- How much balance is needed in your sport in order for your strength to be expressed? Many things can challenge our balance in sports:
    – *Angles of force:* In fencing, the arm movements require a variety of angles. The legs and feet require fewer angles, but they are specialized.
    – *Collision impact:* The fencer must be prepared for occasional, minor collision impact.
    – *Foot slippage:* In fencing, foot slippage is (usually) limited.
    – *Quick starts, stops, and changes of direction:* In fencing there are constant quick starts and stops.

In fact, there are many types of strength but they fall within two main categories of static and dynamic strength. Static means non-moving and is the ability to apply force against a non-moving resistance; another word for static is isometric. Static strength is of limited interest to athletes because the fundamentals of all athletic movements require the levers to move dynamically. Even so, certain areas

STRENGTH AND CONDITIONING

of the body need to be fixed or held close to fixed positions during movements in order to maintain posture.

Dynamic strength is much more complex because there are many ways of moving and the type of strength involved must relate to the type of movement. The body can move quickly or slowly, the pattern and the speed of movement of the relevant body parts may vary, the body parts may be accelerating or decelerating. General strength endurance is the ability to move a resistance, which may only be the body weight, for prolonged periods. Any activity lasting longer than ten to fifteen seconds requires this, since the immediate energy production takes place in the muscles. Local strength endurance is the ability to perform prolonged work against resistance, in a much localized area of the body. (Winch, 2004)

James (2006, pp.14–15) has some useful advice for youth training and training women. Great care is required when training children and heavy lifting should be avoided. Stay away from extremes of heat and humidity because children sweat less, produce more heat per body mass than adults and tend to adapt to heat more slowly. Remember that, when fencing, children will usually wear quite a lot of clothing. It is important not to train hard and for too long, because young athletes are still growing. It is easy for them to develop stress fractures, repetitive use injuries and damage growing joint surfaces. Children do not require a lot of exercise to make their muscles grow, and extreme exhaustion can affect their growth.

As children grow into adulthood these precautions still apply but they will in time graduate to more adult forms of training. While they are growing, continue to avoid heavy lifting or the more demanding forms of plyometrics. Some weightlifting (under expert guidance) is necessary as a preparation for strength training; for skill, rather than muscle building. Women athletes tend to have more injuries than their male counterparts, mainly from joint instability and postural problems. This is because women are likely to be more flexible than men. The simple solution to this is strength training so their nerves and muscles can be taught to provide more stability.

'MUST DO' FREE EXERCISES

- Power clean
- Power snatch
- Back squat
- Front squat
- Squat to toes
- Leg extension (normally performed using a suitable machine)
- Leg biceps curl (normally performed using a suitable machine)
- Bench press
- Press behind neck
- Arm biceps curl
- Lateral pull down (normally performed using a suitable machine)
- Bent-over rowing
- Upright rowing

(Winch, 2005, pp.143–144)

STRENGTH AND CONDITIONING

Basic Weightlifting

Free weights tend to be better at producing functional strength than machines because they challenge your balance and the stability of your joints. With a machine, you are pushing a weight on a track, usually up and down. Hence, the muscles that would keep a real-life load from going left or right, forward or back, do not operate during the lift; this preparation can only be done with free weights. (James, 2006) 'Machines are in some sense foolproof. But if used properly, free weights are safe and they are much more effective. The keys to safe use of free weights are: don't lift more than you can handle *with good form*, don't lift to exhaustion (just to loss of good form), and always work with a spotter, someone who can help you with the weight if you can't control it or if you become too weak to continue.' (James, 2006, p.38)

Winch (2005, p.143) suggests: 'There are a number of universal exercises which, if used properly, will give the rapid all-round strength improvement required to improve power and performance during the competitive life of an athlete.' These are listed in the panel 'Must Do' Free Exercises.

The power clean has been described as an advanced exercise, not suitable for a beginner or someone returning from a lay-off. (James, 2006, p.132) The following is a description of the clean lift, which may in time be progressed to the power clean.

…pushing down on the floor, pulling the elbows straight up towards the ceiling and pointing the toes…

…relaxing the ankles, flexing the knees and cradling the weight on front of the shoulders. (James, 2006, p.63)

LEFT: *In the power clean, the lift is done by flexing the knees with the arms hanging down…*

STRENGTH AND CONDITIONING

For the clean lift, begin by flexing the knees, with the arms hanging down. Push on the floor. Pull the elbows straight up towards the ceiling and point the toes. Relax the ankles, flex the knees, drop the elbows and cradle the weight on the front of the shoulders. This is done at a quick pace so that one part of the lift feeds energy into the next. The main emphasis here is up and should feel like doing a combination of jumping up and pulling up. (James, 2006)

Although not appearing on Winch's list, the dead lift is another useful exercise, which follows.

...letting the bar hang straight down from the shoulders. (James, 2006, p.62)

A dead lift begins with the barbell on the floor, with the shin almost touching the bar. (James, 2006, p.62)

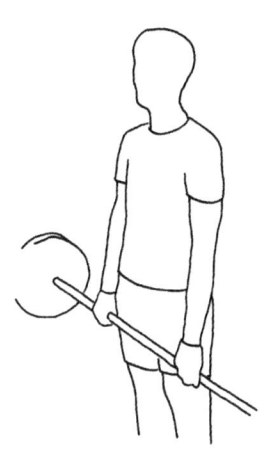

For the dead lift, begin with the barbell on the floor with your shins almost touching the bar. Grab the bar and stand up, letting the bar hang straight down from the shoulders, and then lower it back to the floor. Try to keep the back straight or a little bent forward, with the head and chest up. Throughout the lift your hips should be above the knees and below the shoulders. Avoid locking the knees before the back is vertical. The back and legs should finish the lift at the same time.

This exercise can also be done as a hanging dead lift where the weight is lowered only as far as the knees, instead of all the way to the floor. (James, 2006)

Lunges

The (non-fencing) lunge that follows uses a medicine ball for added weight.

LEFT: *Grab the bar and stand up...*

STRENGTH AND CONDITIONING

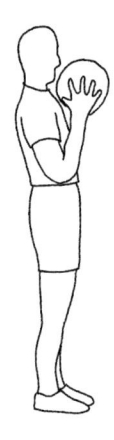

To do this lunging exercise, begin by standing with a medicine ball in front of your chin. (James, 2006, p.64)

Step forward and drop down, keeping the front knee at about 90 degrees. (James, 2006, p.64)

Stand with the ball In front of your chin, then step forward and drop down. Stay upright and keep the hips level, with the front knee at approximately 90 degrees. Push backward and stand up, returning to the start position. Holding the medicine ball in this way exercises the muscles that rotate the shoulders. This lunge can also be done with body weight alone or with dumb-bells.

Each knee should point in the same direction as the attached, the calf near perpendicular to the floor, and the body upright, rather than lying on the front thigh. Try to go in and out of the lunge with a minimum of hip wobble or tilt.

To do the walking lunge, step forward into the lunge position. Then, rather than stepping backward out of the lunge to a standing position, bring the back foot forward until it is beside the front foot and you are standing. Repeat this process, alternating legs and moving across the room. Lunging with hands out to the sides to aid balance is easiest. Lunging with hands on hips is more challenging. The walking lunge can also be practised going backward.

Now do a lunge with a twist. As you step out into the lunge, move the ball in a semicircle over your head. When you settle in the full lunge, the ball will have reached the other side of your body. As you step back out of the lunge, move the ball in the opposite semicircular motion, and finish in the standing position where you started. Ensure that the upper body is vertical throughout. This exercise can be made a little easier by twisting with a smaller ball. This exercise integrates the movements of the torso (moving a medicine ball from side to side) with the lunge, changing the centre of balance as the exercise progresses. Fencers are often required to combine upper and lower body skills that they may have practised separately. (James, 2006)

James (2006, p.87) makes the point that 'Every change presents a learning opportunity for the nervous system. For example, an athlete may be very adept at the walking lunge, but immediately display degraded form when trying to do it backward. To the eye, forward and backward may seem essentially the same because they are mirror images of the same move. But for the body, the backward move is a completely new skill.'

STRENGTH AND CONDITIONING

Jumps

First, bend the legs steadily...

...then jump. (James, 2006, p.126)

A squat jump can be done in two ways. First, to bend the legs steadily and then jump; this is not plyometric. Secondly, to dip sharply and respond as rapidly as possible; this is plyometric. It is essential to bend the limb rapidly and respond even faster. Plyometrics involves the prior rapid stretching of the muscle before contraction. (Winch, 2004) Because of the explosive and stressful nature of plyometrics, only short sessions are used, because tiredness can lead to injury. (Winch, 2005) The basic thinking behind the plyometric approach to training is that maximum tension develops when active muscle is stretched quickly. The faster a muscle is forced to lengthen, the greater the tension it exerts. A concentric contraction of a muscle is much stronger if it immediately follows an eccentric contraction of the same muscle. (Hazeldine, 1985) All movement is accomplished by what is referred to as 'muscle contraction' but despite this name, muscles do not get shorter every time. Contraction where the muscle gets shorter is called 'concentric contraction' and where the muscle lengthens it is called 'eccentric contraction'. (James, 2006)

Plyometric jumps can be categorized by order difficulty, starting with the easiest first: level jumps, box jumps and depth jumps. Level jumps always begin and end on the same level. With box jumps, the athlete jumps from a lower to a higher level and back. Depth jumps are the opposite of box jumps. The athlete jumps down from a box on to the floor, which allows the tendons in the leg to stretch and absorb the falling energy, and after momentary contact with the floor, jumps upward as high as possible. Fencing makes only occasional use of vertical leaps, so level jumps are the most effective type of plyometric jump training; but box and depth jumps improve the springing capability of the muscles, which can also be a useful preparation for fencing. (James, 2006)

STRENGTH AND CONDITIONING

What follow next are explanations of the lunge jump and box jump.

For a lunge jump, begin in the (non-fencing) lunge exercise position. (James, 2006, p.123)

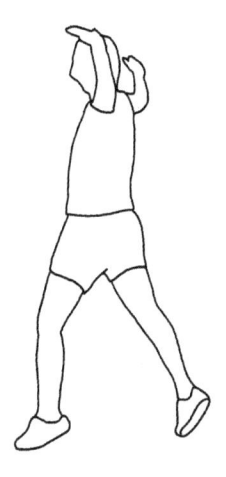

Jump upwards, then land in the starting position. (James, 2006, p.123)

For a lunge jump, begin in the (non-fencing) lunge exercise position. Jump upwards and land in the same start position. Repeat an equal number of times with each leg leading. Keep the upper body between the feet during the leap. The athlete's side-to-side stability will be challenged on landing.

A natural progression from this is the scissors lunge jump, where the legs pass by each other in mid-air, like scissors, and the athlete lands in the lunge position with the legs reversed. (James, 2006)

For a box jump, begin facing a low jumping platform with feet parallel, positioned under the hips. (James, 2006, p.127)

Next, squat down, immediately springing up and forward...

STRENGTH AND CONDITIONING

...landing on the platform in a balanced semi-squat position. (James, 2006, p.127)

For a box jump, begin facing a low jumping platform with feet parallel, positioned under the hips. Next, squat down, immediately springing up and forward, landing on the platform in a balanced semi-squat position, retaining an upright posture throughout. Then hop backward and return to the floor. This exercise is an advanced form of the squat. (James, 2006)

Fencing Exercises Using Body Weight

In the photographs of team fencing that follow the atmosphere is intense. Team matches such as this form an important part of the fencing calendar and may be found in countries around the world. Additional photographs can be found at the end of this chapter. Fencers at all levels have to manoeuvre their own body weight over periods of time and through some quite difficult situations.

New fencers tend to build up strength initially using just body weight; later they are likely to go on to some form of specific weights programme. (Paul, et al., 2012) It is probably useful at this stage to mention some typical fencing exercises using body weight. There are many possibilities and these are just a few.

(a) These lunging exercises are designed to strengthen and coordinate the muscles of the arms and legs and should be carried out rhythmically:

- In the lunge position, press the body weight down between the legs and relax. Rest the arms.
- Returning to the lunge position, stretch the front leg fully and then rock on the heel, at the same time bending the rear knee, transferring body weight to the rear, and simultaneously bringing up the rear arm. Then reverse this action, returning to the lunge position. Try sitting down a little further on to the rear leg each time.
- Repeat the previous exercise but this time thrust off the front foot, making sure that the thrust comes from the heel of the front foot. Immediately thrust from the rear foot before the front foot comes to rest in the on guard position, then return to the lunge. Keep the front foot in line with the knee on the recovery, toes up.
- From the lunge bring the rear foot forward into the on guard position. Reverse this action back into the lunge. Keep the same angle in the front leg all the time so that the whole body weight is taken on the leg. (Anderson, 1973, pp. 89-91)

53

STRENGTH AND CONDITIONING

England 15 Scotland 23 at the Five Nations Tournament, Edinburgh, 2013.

England 25 Scotland 35 at the Five Nations Tournament, Edinburgh, 2013.

STRENGTH AND CONDITIONING

England 37 Scotland 42 at the Five Nations Tournament, Edinburgh, 2013.

England 39 Scotland 44 at the Five Nations Tournament, Edinburgh, 2013.

STRENGTH AND CONDITIONING

England 40 Scotland 45, the final result of the match, at the Five Nations Tournament, Edinburgh, 2013.

(b) Various hopping exercises:

- You can start by hopping on both feet. While in mid-air, clap hands on the front of the body or alternately on the front and behind the body; two, three or four times. Next, hop on both feet and simultaneously twist the trunk of the body at the hips.
- Hop with the feet apart, landing alternately on one foot then the other, bending the knee on landing to take up a semi-lunge position.
- Try hopping from a closed stance to a

STRENGTH AND CONDITIONING

straddle and back, lifting the arms to shoulder height on landing, altering the size and speed of the straddle, occasionally pausing at a chosen point. This can also be done by alternating a single lifted arm to shoulder height on either side on landing or alternating one arm at shoulder height with the other lifted overhead, rocking between the two positions each time on landing.

- Practise hopping on the non-dominant foot. Pull the other knee up on the front of the corresponding shoulder or place the other foot on the knee of the supporting leg and twist the trunk of the body at the hips while hopping. Alternatively, circle the leg forward and backward while in the air.

(Lukovich, 1998; 2013)

Fencers shake hands at the end of a match at the Five Nations Tournament, Edinburgh, 2013.

STRENGTH AND CONDITIONING

(c) Wall press-ups:

- Stand at arm's length from a wall. Place your palms hands on the wall, at shoulder height, with the feet slightly apart. Keep the feet flat on the floor and allow the elbows to bend until the forehead touches the wall, then push back on the palms until you return to the start position. Breathe out while the arms are bending and breathe in while returning to the upright position.
- This time, place the palms of your ands lower, close as you can get to waist height, and then proceed as before. This can also be done using the back of a chair, so long as it is held secure.

(Simmonds and Morton, 1997)

(d) Jump from one leg:

- Step on to a bench so your upper leg is almost parallel to the floor. Jump straight up using that leg. Push off, straightening the foot, pushing off with your toes. Then do the other leg.

(Volkmann, 1997)

Main Points

- Conditioning is the work needed to prepare for the stresses and strains of training and competition. Using weights is a very efficient way of conditioning your body.
- Core stability is about keeping the correct posture during athletic performance. Basic weight training has a high core conditioning element.
- The interval between stimulus and response is called 'reaction time'.
- Training optimizes performance by developing healthy muscle responses that can cope with unstable situations.
- There are many types of 'strength'. The category most applicable to fencing is 'dynamic strength', which is complex and involves different types of movement.
- General strength endurance is the ability to move a resistance (such as your body weight) for prolonged periods. Local strength endurance is the ability to perform prolonged work against resistance in a much localized area of the body (lunging).
- Free weights challenge your balance and the stability of your joints. Lift only what you can handle with 'good form'.
- Plyometrics involves the prior rapid stretching before contraction. This is because a 'concentric contraction', where the muscle gets shorter, is much stronger if it immediately follows an 'eccentric contraction', where the same muscle lengthens.

CHAPTER THREE

NUTRITION

Food is fuel – not a treat, not a comfort blanket.

(Beasley, in Paul, et al., 2012, p.42)

What you eat greatly influences your ability to train hard, fight hard and recover quickly. (Paul, et al., 2012) Diet affects performance.

(Bean, 2009) The body cannot create or lose energy, it can only transform energy. Thus, the energy contained in food is transformed into biological energy. (Dunford, 2010) The complex character of fencing training can lead to great diversity in the amount of energy expenditure required. Mental processes are

Gioia Marzocca of Italy gets a pep talk from her coach at the Senior Women's Sabre 'A' Grade, London, 2011. (Photo: Graham Morrison)

NUTRITION

also crucial. Consequently, a fencer's diet should counteract fatigue of the central nervous system as well as of the muscles. (Borysiuk, 2009)

Hazeldine and Cadman (1984, pp.19–20) say: 'The right diet is essential to keep the performer's body fuelled correctly. The muscles must receive a good supply of fats and carbohydrates to produce energy, while proteins are needed to build the muscles up. Essential water and minerals are lost through sweating, and must be replaced by taking suitable amounts of water plus a variety of minerals. Lastly, vitamins are required to regulate the body's chemical reactions – reactions that are speeded up when the body is active.' Vitamins are needed in tiny amounts for growth, health and physical well-being. Our bodies are unable to make vitamins, so they need to be supplied in our diet. (Bean, 2009)

To control appetite, regulate blood sugar level and build lean body mass you must eat five to six small-medium sized meals or snacks a day. That means you need to eat on average every three hours: effectively 'grazing' throughout the day. Frequently digesting food cranks up your metabolism and burns more calories every time you eat. (Verstegen and Williams, 2005)

Generally speaking, if a person feels well and is neither too fat nor too thin, then their nutrition is probably about right. (Hazeldine, 1985) That being said, any fencer planning to make substantial changes to their diet should take professional advice, which takes into account their previous medical history, age and any other relevant factors, before settling on any particular course of action.

Principal Nutrients

The principal nutrients used by the body are carbohydrates, fats and proteins. Many foods are a mixture of all three. (Dunford, 2010) Carbohydrates, fats and proteins are all capable of providing energy for exercise and can be transported to and broken down in muscle cells. Alcohol produces calories but cannot be used directly by muscles for energy during exercise. Only the liver has enzymes needed to break down alcohol, which is done at a fixed speed. (Bean, 2009) Vitamins do not provide energy, although some are involved in the release of energy from food. (Griffin, 2002) While intense exercise increases the requirement for several vitamins and minerals, there is no need for supplements so long as you are eating a balanced diet. (Bean, 2009)

A good example of how a balanced diet translates into actual food is shown in the 'Food Pyramid for Athletes' produced by the Swiss Society for Nutrition. Each food group provides some, but not all, of the nutrients required to keep fit and healthy. You should aim to eat a variety of foods within each group and roughly the recommended number of portions each day. Foods in the lower areas of the pyramid – fruit, vegetables and carbohydrate-rich foods – should form the main part of the diet; while those at the top should be eaten in smaller quantities. Each food group is equally important and you need to get the correct balance. (Bean, 2003) It is important to ensure that carbohydrates come from a wide range of wholesome foods, because certain vitamins and minerals are necessary for the body to convert carbohydrates into energy. (Holt, 2004)

Carbohydrate

Borysiuk (2009, p.117) advises that: 'Carbohydrates are of crucial significance in endurance-speed sports such as fencing… The larger the fencer's carbohydrate stores, the greater his or her efficiency.' Carbohydrates are what give you strength and stamina. They are also

Food pyramid for athletes. (Courtesy Swiss Forum for Sports Nutrition)

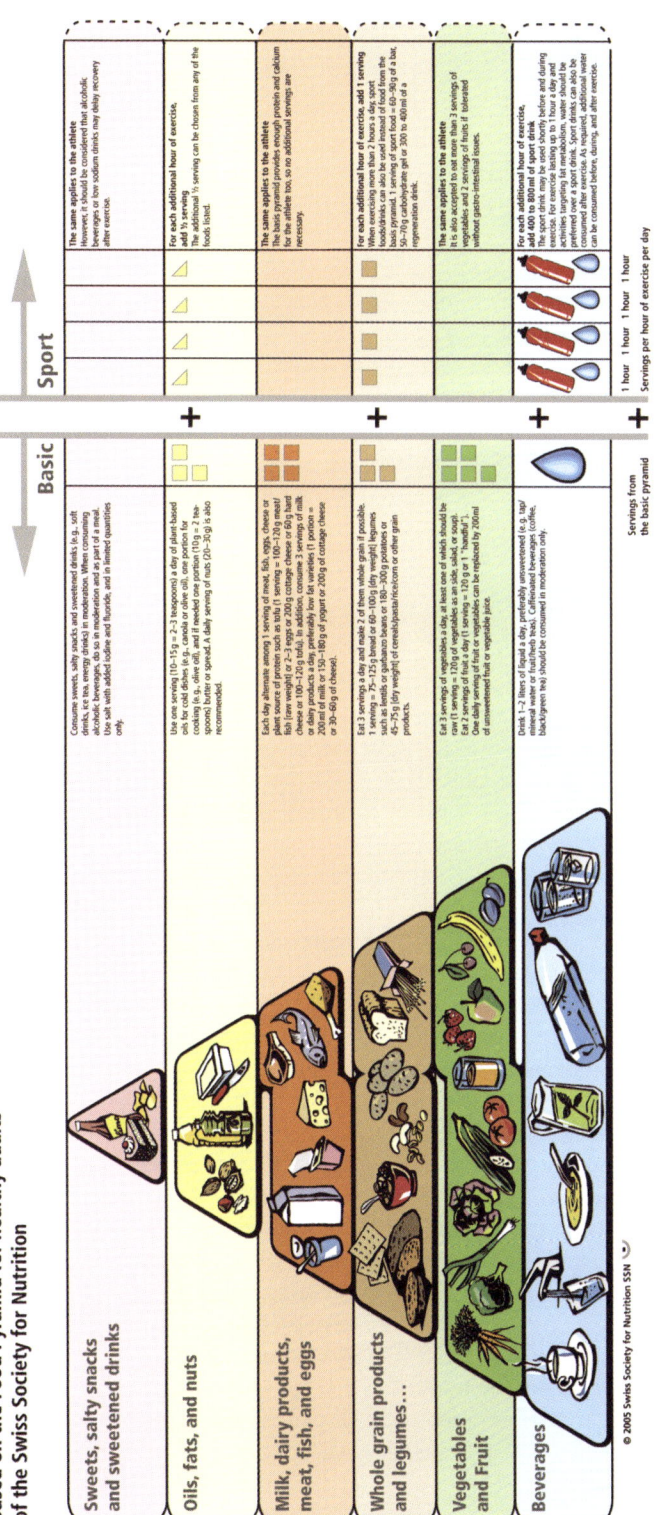

NUTRITION

the best source of energy for the nerves and the brain. (Muliar, 2001) It has been suggested there is evidence that athletes on high-carbohydrate diets achieve significantly better results compared with those on low-carbohydrate diets. (Bean, 2002, p.15) While fat and protein can also provide fuel during aerobic activities, it is carbohydrate alone that is burned during the earlier stages of exercise and also during anaerobic (very high-intensity, explosive) activities. (Bean, 2002)

Most carbohydrates in the diet, with the exception of milk, come from plants and are found in food as sugars, starches and fibre. In the body, carbohydrates are found as glucose and glycogen. Glucose is blood sugar and glycogen is the storage form of carbohydrate found in the muscles and liver. (Griffin, 2002; Dunford, 2010) Glycogen is stored along with about three times its own weight in water. Three times more glycogen is stored in the muscles than in the liver. The purpose of liver glycogen is to maintain steady blood sugar levels. When blood glucose dips, glycogen in the liver breaks down to release glucose into the bloodstream. The purpose of muscle glycogen is to fuel muscle activity. (Bean, 2009) Exercising muscle prefers to use muscle glycogen if it is available. (Dunford, 2010)

High glycogen levels help to maintain a higher training intensity for longer and thus improve sporting performance. (Bean, 2002) On a high-carbohydrate diet the storage of glycogen is two times larger than in athletes on a low-carbohydrate diet. An athlete on a diet rich in carbohydrates can replenish his/her stored glycogen in twenty-four hours, while an athlete on a low-carbohydrate diet may take forty-eight hours or more. (Borysiuk, 2009) However, it should be noted that once glycogen stores are depleted, the body draws on its protein stores, to the detriment of muscle mass. Fat deposits can also be drawn on for energy. (Muliar, 2001)

Some carbohydrates are quickly absorbed, producing a rapid rise in blood sugar. Such foods give a quick energy boost. Others are absorbed more slowly, producing a smaller but more prolonged rise in blood sugar. Bananas, sugar, potatoes and rice produce a rapid rise in blood sugar. They are quickly digested and absorbed. Pulses, oats and most fruit produce a slower blood sugar rise. (Bean, 2002)

Fat

Fat is the second most important source of energy for the human body, after carbohydrate, but is less efficient. (Borysiuk, 2009) A small amount is essential for good health. (Bean, 2002) It plays an important role in the diet of a physically active person, is the primary source of energy at rest, and is twice as energy-dense as carbohydrate or protein. It also provides essential fatty acids and fat-soluble vitamins that our bodies need. (Manore, Meyer and Thompson, 2009) Fat is stored in almost every region of the body. A small amount is stored in the muscles but the majority is stored around the muscles and beneath the skin. (Bean, 2009) At rest approximately 75 to 80 per cent of the energy needed to keep the body alive, comes from fat. The remainder comes mainly from carbohydrate. Although this percentage is (apparently) high, the total amount of energy being consumed is quite low. (Dunford, 2010)

The fat you eat is readily converted into body fat. It does not satisfy the appetite as well as carbohydrate or protein, so it is easy to overeat fatty foods without feeling full. (Bean, 2002) Some fats have been labelled as 'good' to indicate that they have been found to reduce the risk of heart disease. (Dunford, 2010) It is important to ensure that you get the right amount of good-quality fats from wholesome food, such as nuts, seeds, avocados, fish and lean meat, while cutting back on less nutritious fatty foods. (Holt, 2004)

NUTRITION

The human body can make most of the type of fats it needs from other fats or raw materials, but that is not the case with omega-3 fats. These are 'essential' fats; the body cannot make them from scratch but obtains them from food. Foods high in omega-3 include fish, vegetable oils, nuts (especially walnuts), flax seeds, flaxseed oil and leafy vegetables. (HSPH, n.d.) Omega-3s may be particularly beneficial for athletes as they help to increase the delivery of oxygen to the muscles, improve endurance and may speed recovery, as well as reduce inflammation and joint stiffness. (Bean, 2009)

Protein

Protein makes up part of the structure of every cell and tissue in the body. On average, it comprises about 20 per cent of your total body weight. It also has the role of maintaining optimal fluid balance in tissues, transporting nutrients in and out of cells, carrying oxygen and regulating blood clotting. (Bean, 2009) The amino acids that make up different proteins are needed by the body for tissue growth, maintenance and repair, as well as for producing antibodies and the enzymes and hormones that regulate many important metabolic processes. The amount of protein that the body needs each day is relatively small. Most protein comes from animal products such as dairy, meat, poultry and seafood. Protein in the muscles is constantly being repaired or remade as it is injured or ages. (Holt, 2004)

Regular exercise increases the amount of protein needed by the body, mostly to repair tissue and grow extra muscle. Dietary proteins are made up of chains of amino acids, nine of which are referred to as 'essential' as they cannot be made in adult bodies, so must come from the diet. Lean animal foods such as red meat, fish, eggs and low-fat dairy products contain all the essential amino acids needed by the human body. However, it is possible for vegetarians to get all the essential amino acids by combining foods from different groups. (Holt, 2004) Skimping on protein can cause fatigue and slow recovery after workouts. (Bean, 2003) Proteins are not stored in the same way as carbohydrate and fat. They form muscle and organ tissue, so are mainly used as building material. They can be broken down to release energy if needed, so muscles and organs represent a large source of potential energy. (Bean, 2009)

Some athletes eat high protein diets in the mistaken belief that extra protein leads to increased strength and muscle mass but it is the stimulation of muscle tissue through exercise that leads to muscle growth. Protein is found in so many foods that most people eat more than they need. This is not harmful because the excess is broken down into fuel, which is either used for energy, stored as fat, or excreted. (Bean, 2009)

Fluid

It has been said that: 'Well-fuelled and well-hydrated athletes reduce their risk of injury during exercise – a risk that increases as individuals become fatigued and lose their ability to concentrate…' (Manore, Meyer and Thompson, 2009, p.2) Hydration helps to keep the body temperature stable. If you become dehydrated during exercise your body will overheat. (Bean, 2003) If you do not replace lost water, the body's core temperature will increase and performance will suffer. As the blood becomes 'thicker', the heart needs to beat faster to pump the blood around the body, and the body is put under greater stress. (Bean, 2002)

Water makes up about 50 to 70 per cent of your body weight. (Holt, 2004) The body produces energy so it can live, breathe and

NUTRITION

move; but only 25 per cent of that energy is actually used for mechanical work. The other 75 per cent is released as heat. To get rid of heat, you sweat. As sweat evaporates, your blood and body cool down. (Kleiner and Greenwood-Robinson, 1996) Unless you have been sweating heavily, electrolyte (mineral salts) loss is less critical than water loss and can easily be replaced by food consumed in your next normal meal. (Bean, 2003)

Muscular movement depends on the presence of water, which is found in the highest concentration in metabolically active tissues such as muscle, and in the lowest amounts in relatively inactive tissue such as fat, skin and some parts of bone. Muscles are controlled by nerves. The electrical stimulation of nerves and the contraction of muscles occur due to the exchange of electrolyte minerals dissolved in water across the nerve and muscle cell membranes. So, if you are low on water, or electrolytes, muscle strength and control can be weakened. The function of the heart depends on muscle stimulation. The electrical impulses in the brain and balance mechanisms are extremely sensitive to the presence of adequate amounts of water.

RECIPES FOR HOMEMADE ISOTONIC DRINKS

50 to 70g glucose or sucrose (ordinary sugar)
One litre warm water
Large pinch of salt (1 to 1.5g)

Warm a small amount of the water and use to dissolve the glucose and salt. Flavour with low-sugar or low-calorie squash (not regular squash as this will upset the balance of carbohydrate). Top up to a litre with water. Mix together, cover and keep chilled in the fridge.

500ml unsweetened fruit juice (for example orange, pineapple, or grapefruit)
500ml water
Large pinch of salt (1 to 1.5g)

Warm a small amount of the water and use this to dissolve the salt. Add the fruit juice and remaining cold water. Mix together, cover and keep chilled in the fridge.

200ml squash (any flavour but not low-sugar or no-added-sugar varieties)
800ml water
Large pinch of salt (1 to 1.5g)

Warm a small amount of the water and use this to dissolve the salt. Add the squash and remaining cold water. Mix together, cover and keep chilled in the fridge.

Make up a new batch of drink every day and throw away any unused drink every twenty-four hours. Keep water bottles very clean. Sugary drinks attract insects and will provide fertile breeding grounds for bacteria. This is important at all times but especially during warm weather.

(Griffin, 2002, p.87)

NUTRITION

Water also forms the make-up of lubricating fluid between your joints. (Kleiner and Greenwood-Robinson, 1996) Water acts as a lubricant that bathes all the tissue and cells in the body. It is a transport medium in which many compounds can be transported to the cells and is also the medium in which waste materials are removed from the body. People with more muscle mass have a higher percentage of water than those with more body fat. As men typically have a higher percentage of lean body mass than women, they typically have a higher percentage of water in their body weight. (Manore, Meyer and Thompson, 2009)

Broadly speaking, there are three different types of carbohydrate drinks. A hypotonic drink, often marketed as 'sports water', contains fewer particles (carbohydrate and electrolytes) per 100 ml than the body's own fluids. An isotonic drink, a typical 'sports drink', contains about the same number of particles (carbohydrate and electrolytes) per 100ml as the body's own fluids. In theory, isotonic drinks provide the ideal compromise between rehydration and refuelling. Relatively easy to make, some examples are included in the panel entitled 'Recipes for Homemade Isotonic Drinks'. A hypertonic drink, such as soft drinks and fizzy drinks, contains more particles (carbohydrate and electrolytes) per 100ml than the body's fluids, because it is more concentrated. (Bean, 2009)

The ideal sports rehydration drink must contain carbohydrate, sodium and water. (Griffin, 2002) It has been suggested (Gisolphi, et al., 1992, cited in Bean, 2009, p.94) that carbohydrate in sports drinks speeds up water absorption. It also provides a useful additional source of energy (Coggan and Coyle, 1987 cited in Bean, 2009, p.94). Sports drinks may be better than water at speeding recovery after exercise. The problem with drinking water is that it dilutes sodium in the blood, reducing thirst and increasing urine output; so you may stop drinking before you are rehydrated. Electrolytes in sports drinks do not have a direct effect on performance. However, sodium in a sports drink does increase the urge to drink and improves palatability. Electrolytes are mineral salts dissolved in the body's fluid; including sodium (previously mentioned), chloride, potassium and magnesium, and help to regulate fluid balance between different body compartments and the volume of fluid in the bloodstream. (Bean, 2009)

Bean (2003, p.30) advises you should: 'Drink before you get thirsty. By the time your thirst mechanism kicks in, you will have lost around 2 per cent of your body weight as water. If you relied on your thirst alone, you would replace only 50 to 75 per cent of what you need.'

With an understanding of how the principal nutrients work, it is possible to develop a better understanding of a nutritional regime for fencing training and competition.

Training Diet

It is important not to exercise on a full stomach or when the stomach is completely empty. As a general rule of thumb allow:

- Approximately one hour for a snack to digest.
- Two to three hours for a small/medium-sized meal to digest.
- Three to four hours for a large meal to digest.

(Bean, 2002)

Examples of the type of things to consume are shown in the panels entitled Pre-Workout Snacks, Before Exercise and Pre-Workout Meals. Pre-workout meals are typically high in

NUTRITION

Pre-Workout Snacks
Fresh fruit
Dried apricots, date or raisins
Smoothie (homemade or ready bought)
Yoghurt
Shake (homemade or meal replacement shake)
Energy or nutrition bar
Cereal bar or breakfast bar
Fruit loaf or raisin bread
Diluted fruit juice

(Bean, 2009, p.32)

Before Exercise
A bowl of cereal with semi-skimmed milk
Two to three slices of toast or a bagel with honey, jam or marmalade
A bowl of pasta with tomato-based sauce
A bowl of porridge with raisins
A cereal bar and a banana
A handful of dried apricots and raisins and a tub of low-fat yoghurt

(Benson, n.d. p.11)

Pre-Workout Meals
Sandwich/roll/bagel/wrap filled with chicken, fish, cheese, egg or peanut butter and salad
Jacket potato with beans, cheese, tuna, coleslaw or chicken
Pasta with tomato-based sauce and cheese and vegetables
Chicken with rice and salad
Vegetable and prawn or tofu stir-fry with noodles or rice
Pilaf or rice salad
Mixed bean hotpot with potatoes
Chicken and vegetable casserole with potatoes
Porridge made with milk
Wholegrain cereal (e.g. bran or wheat flakes, muesli or Weetabix) with milk or yoghurt
Fish and potato pie

(Bean, 2009, p.32)

During Exercise
A banana with regular sips of water
Oranges at breaks
Fruit bar and cereal bar or a handful of raisins
Regular sips of an isotonic sports drink
50/50 mixture of fruit juice and water or a diluted standard squash

(Benson, n.d., p.11)

NUTRITION

Post-Exercise Snacks
A meal replacement shake (a balanced mixture of maltodextrin, sugar and whey protein together with vitamins and minerals)
One to two portions of fresh fruit with a drink of milk
One or two cartons of yoghurt
A smoothie (crushed fresh fruit whizzed in a blender)
A homemade milkshake (milk with fresh fruit or yoghurt)
A yoghurt drink
A sports bar (containing carbohydrate and protein)
A sandwich/bagel/roll/wrap filled with lean protein – tuna, chicken, cottage cheese, peanut butter or egg
A handful of dried fruit and nuts
A few rice cakes with jam or peanut butter and cottage cheese
A bowl of wholegrain cereal with milk
A bowl of porridge made with milk
Jacket potato with tuna, baked beans or cottage cheese

(Bean, 2009, p.37)

A sandwich or roll
A bagel with strawberry jam or honey and banana
A cereal bar and a tub of low-fat yoghurt
A bowl of cereal with semi-skimmed milk
Three jaffa cakes and a milkshake made from semi-skimmed milk

(Paterson, n.d., p.15)

After Exercise Meals
Beef and couscous salad. Baked potato with chilli beef and beans and salad on the side
Pork with plum sauce
Beef (or pork or chicken) stir-fry with vegetables and rice
Lamb wraps
Beef and spinach lasagne
Baked beans on toast (throw in some frozen peas and corn for veg)

(Paterson, n.d., p.15)

NUTRITION

carbohydrate, moderate in protein and relatively low in fat because the latter is digested more slowly than either carbohydrate or protein. (Dunford, 2010)

If doing intense exercise for more than one hour you can either get carbohydrate from a sports drink or carbohydrate-rich food that is easy to digest. It is better to eat small amounts at intervals, rather than a lot at once. It is also important to keep fully hydrated. (Bupa, n.d.) Examples of what to consume are shown in the panel entitled During Exercise.

Bean (2003, p.37) says that during a workout: 'The American College of Sports Medicine and Dietetics Association recommends drinking around 150 to 350ml (of fluid) every fifteen to twenty minutes. You should start drinking early during your workout as it takes about thirty minutes for the fluid to be absorbed into your bloodstream.' For workouts lasting less than one hour, water is all that is required. It is absorbed relatively fast into the bloodstream and keeps the body hydrated. For more than one hour, drinks containing carbohydrates are often a better choice than plain water. The sugars they contain not only provide fuel for exercising muscle, but also speed up the absorption of water into the bloodstream. (Bean, 2003)

Griffin (2002, p.88) advises that: 'Sweat loss can be estimated by weighing before and after the training session. Weighing should be done naked or, if this is not practical, wearing the minimum of dry clothing with the body towelled down. The aim is to make the weighing conditions at both times as similar as possible, so sweaty clothing should not be worn for the post-training weighing… Reliable scales should be used, ideally weighing to the nearest 100g.' Work on the basis that one litre of sweat is roughly equivalent to one kilogram of body weight loss. (Bean, 2009)

Researchers (IAAF, 2007; Shirreffs et al., 2004; Shirreffs et al., 1996, cited in Bean, 2009, p.91) recommend that you should consume approx. 1.2 to 1.5 times the weight of fluid lost during exercise. This is because most athletes will finish a training session with a fluid deficit, which should be rectified over a four to six-hour post-exercise period.

After an intensive workout, you may not feel hungry for about an hour. It is only after your metabolism and circulation return to normal that you will feel hungry. (Muliar, 2001) A post-exercise 'carbohydrate window', which enables speedy glycogen recovery, occurs fifteen to thirty minutes after exercise. (Borysiuk, 2009, p.124) For about two hours after exercise, glycogen is restored at a faster rate than normal: in fact, almost one and a half times faster. It is during this time that muscle cells are more permeable to glucose. This is because hormones and enzymes are released that favour the uptake of glucose and the formation of glycogen. The best types of carbohydrates to ingest during this period are those that are absorbed rapidly into the body: both solid and liquid are equally effective. (Bean, 2002; Dunford, 2010)

Examples of things to consume are shown in the panels entitled Post-Exercise Snacks and After Exercise Meals.

Competition Diet

The aim of pre-event meals in the run-up to a competition is to top up the body's glycogen stores during the twenty-four to thirty-six hours before an event, by consuming low-fat, high-carbohydrate meals and reducing physical activity. Avoid drinking alcohol for at least two days beforehand, because it can disturb the muscles' use of carbohydrate for fuel. (Holt, 2004) The day before a competition you should rest or do only very

NUTRITION

Jerry Chang of the USA sips fluid at the Eden Cup Junior 'A' Grade men's individual foil, London, 2013. (Photo: Graham Morrison)

NUTRITION

Great Britain's Kristjan Archer takes a drink at the Leon Paul Cup men's individual foil, London, 2013. (Photo: Graham Morrison)

NUTRITION

light exercise. Eat a substantial supper high in carbohydrate to top up muscle glycogen stores. Stick to plain foods, such as pasta, potatoes and rice, and keep the fat content of the meal to a minimum. (Bean, 2002)

Liver glycogen plays a major role in maintaining blood glucose levels throughout the night and a morning meal before a competition helps replenish glycogen stores. (Manore, Meyer and Thompson, 2009) If you normally drink tea or coffee, then include this with your meal to avoid any caffeine withdrawal symptoms but drink more water to compensate for the diuretic effect of caffeine. (Holt, 2004)

Bean (2002, pp.102–104) recommends when competing in the morning you should eat a light breakfast or snack high in carbohydrate. Drink 250 to 500ml of fluid two hours before the event, followed by 125 to 250ml immediately before the event. Choose water or an isotonic sports drink. Fencers will often be seen at a competition topping up with water or a sports drink, with small regular sips.

Some breakfast suggestions are shown in the panel entitled Pre-Competition Breakfast.

Carbohydrate ingestion should begin early in an event to ensure that adequate reserves are available in the later stages. If athletes wait until the onset of fatigue before consuming carbohydrate, they may be unable to absorb it rapidly enough to avoid the problem. (Manore, Meyer and Thompson, 2009) Aim to eat little and often and avoid long gaps. Take a good supply of snacks and drinks such as:

- Sandwiches
- Bread, bagels, buns
- Fresh fruit
- Low-fat yoghurt, rice pudding, fromage frais
- Muffins
- Snack bars and cookies
- Homemade cakes
- Rice cakes
- Energy bars and fruit bars
- Low-crackers and biscuits (e.g. fig rolls)
- Diluted squash or fruit juice
- Sports drinks (homemade or commercial)
- Water
- Ready-to-drink meal replacement shakes

(Bean, 2002)

It should be possible to get an idea of the range of approximate fluid requirements for an individual during the course of a fencing competition. What follows are theoretic assumptions only and no training decisions should be made on the basis of these fairly rudimentary calculations. However, this should give a general indication of the extent of hydration required.

As outlined earlier, it has been recommended an individual drinks 250 to 500ml of fluid two hours before the event, followed by 125 to 250ml immediately before it. Secondly, it has been suggested by The American College of Sports Medicine and Dietetics Association, that during exercise, athletes should drink around 150 to 350ml of fluid every fifteen to twenty minutes. (cited in Bean, 2003, p.37)

Pre-Competition Breakfast

One bowl of breakfast cereal (e.g. Cornflakes, Weetabix)
Low-fat milk
Toast with jam or honey
Fresh fruit
Water
or
Toast, English muffins, pancakes or bagels with honey
Fruit juice and water

(Bean, 2002, p.103)

71

NUTRITION

Let us assume that in the early stages there are two poules of seven participants. Each person is fencing six bouts in each poule, with each bout lasting up to three minutes. This equates to eighteen minutes of fairly continuous exercise per poule. The minimum estimated fluid requirement for each poule can be calculated as (eighteen minutes based on 150ml for twenty minutes) – 135ml, the maximum estimated fluid requirement for each poule can be calculated as (eighteen minutes based on 350ml for fifteen minutes) – 420ml.

We can assume the participant will face up to three fencing periods of three minutes during the direct elimination (DE) rounds (foil and épée), i.e. a total of nine minutes. The minimum estimated fluid requirement for each round can be calculated as (nine minutes based on 150ml for twenty minutes) – 67.5ml. The maximum estimated fluid requirement for each round can be calculated as (nine minutes based on 350ml for fifteen minutes) – 210ml. This information is summarized in the two figures entitled Theoretical Hydration Cycle for a Fencing Competition. Additional water will be required for the periods between fencing, including warm-ups, which is not shown.

Refuel and rehydrate as soon as possible after an event. Drink at least 500ml of water or sports drink immediately afterwards and continue drinking at regular intervals. Your post-event meal should be high in carbohydrate and contain moderate amounts of fat and protein. (Bean, 2002) Some suggestions for post-event recovery foods are shown in the panels entitled Recovery Snacks Containing 50g of Carbohydrate and Suitable Post-Event Meals. Most athletes will finish a fencing competition with a fluid deficit, which should be rectified over a four- to six-hour post-exercise period.

Beasley (in Paul, et al., 2012, p.42) advises that, after a competition, a good mix of carbohydrates, proteins, essential fats and micronutrients rich in vitamins, minerals and antioxidants are what is required.

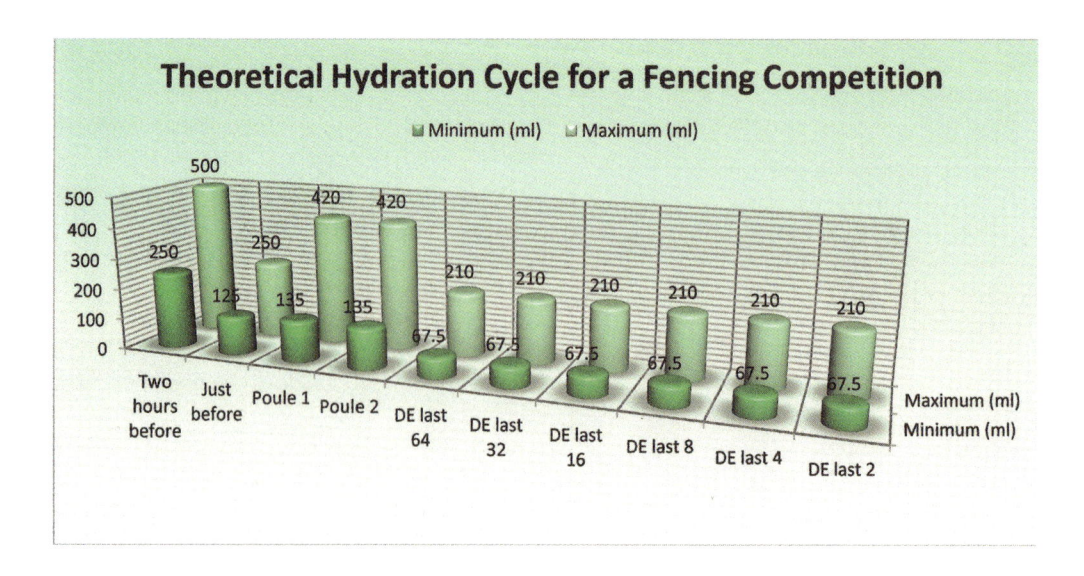

Theoretical hydration cycle for a fencing competition. (1)

NUTRITION

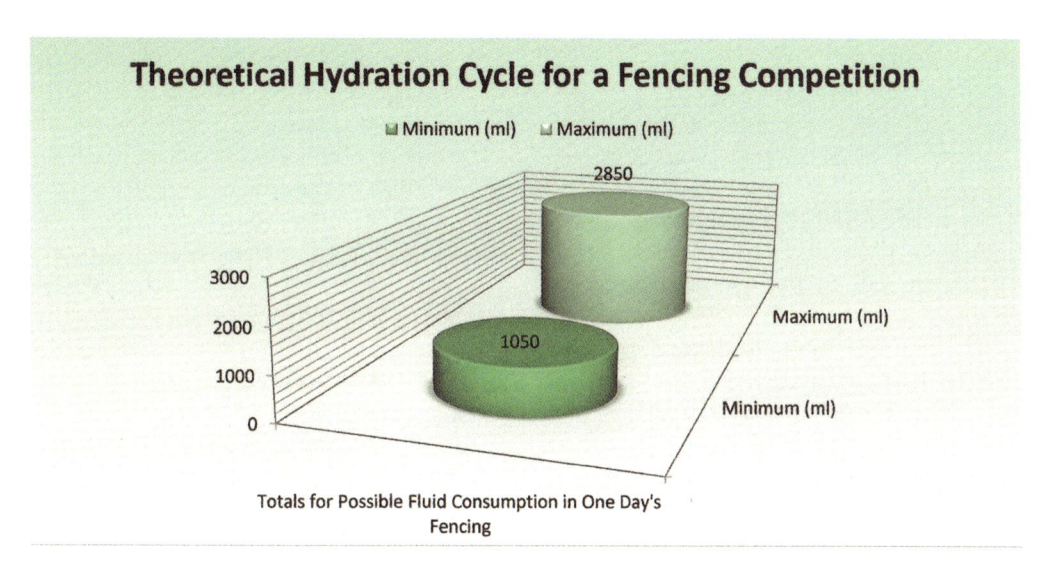

Theoretical Hydration Cycle for a Fencing Competition

Minimum (ml): 1050
Maximum (ml): 2850

Totals for Possible Fluid Consumption in One Day's Fencing

Theoretical hydration cycle for a fencing competition. (2) (Totals for Possible Fluid Consumption in One Day's Fencing.)

Recovery Snacks Containing 50g of Carbohydrate
825 to 1,000ml sports drink
500ml orange juice, soft drink (soda) or flavoured mineral water
Two low-fat breakfast cereal bars
Three pieces of fruit, such as a banana, apple and pear
60g packet of jelly beans or jelly babies
Two 200g cartons of low-fat fruit yoghurt
A jam sandwich (two thick slices of bread with lots of jam and no margarine)
A large bread roll with jam or mashed banana filling
A cup of thick vegetable soup with a large bread roll
A salad sandwich with a slice of lean meat or reduced-fat cheese and a piece of fruit
Two cups of breakfast cereal with low-fat milk
Fresh or tinned fruit salad with low-fat yoghurt

(Holt, 2004, p.25)

Suitable Post-Event Meals
Thick-crust pizza with vegetable topping
Jacket potato filled with beans, fish, chicken or cheese
Rice dishes such as risotto or rice salad
Pasta dishes (avoid creamy sauces)
Low-fat or vegetable lasagne
Pasta salads

(Bean, 2002, p.105)

NUTRITION

Main Points

- A suitable diet counteracts fatigue of the central nervous system, as well as of the muscles.
- For athletes, it is better to consume several small-medium sized meals or snacks a day.
- Consult your doctor if you plan to make substantial changes to your diet.
- The principal nutrients of the body are carbohydrates, fats and proteins.
- Carbohydrates are of crucial importance in endurance sports such as fencing because they are stored in the muscles (as glycogen) and fuel muscle activity.
- Fats are the second most important source of energy after carbohydrate and provide essential fatty acids and fat-soluble vitamins for the body. Some are 'essential' as they can only come from the diet.
- Regular exercise increases the need for proteins, which the body uses to repair tissue and grow extra muscle. Proteins are made up of amino acids, nine of which are 'essential' as they can only come from the diet.
- The body needs water in order to function properly. Always exercise fully hydrated and drink before you get thirsty.
- Never exercise on a full stomach or when the stomach is completely empty and always allow sufficient time for food to digest. For a workout lasting less than one hour, water is sufficient. For a workout lasting more than one hour, a drink containing carbohydrate is often a better option. Remember that glycogen is restored faster in the period following intense exercise.
- A cycle of nutrition/hydration should be observed before, during and after every fencing competition.

Eden Cup Junior 'A' Grade men's individual foil semi-final, London, 2013. Francesco Ingargiola of Italy, left, takes on Jerry Chang of the USA. Ingargiola won 15/9. (Photo: Graham Morrison)

NUTRITION

Eden Cup Junior 'A' Grade men's individual foil final, London, 2013. France's Maximilien Chastanet, left, on his way to a 15/9 defeat against Francesco Ingargiola of Italy.

CHAPTER FOUR

TALENT OR HARD WORK?

Nature may provide us with the initial foundations, but it is the quality of the nurturing that generates the potential to stretch the limits of human performance.

(Whyte, 2012)

If you wish to see some high-performance fencers in action, then look no further than the latter stages of a good 'open' competition. In the photographs that follow, not only are the fencers physically dynamic but in order to succeed, their thinking processes need to be every bit as adept.

All these fencers are highly motivated. Their abilities are almost certainly the result of years of training and competition experience, but how do fencers like this set out on the road to high performance? Is it something they learn or something they are born with?

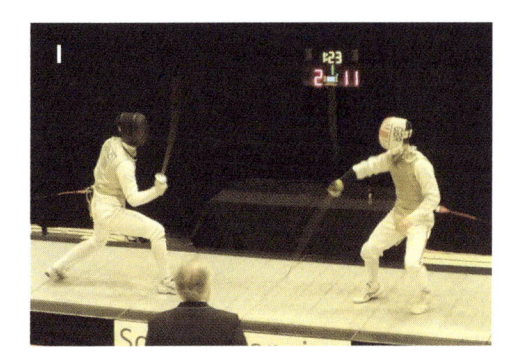

Keith Cook (right) lowers his blade briefly and then lifts. Note how his rear foot moves back slightly, as though he is thinking about retreating. Suddenly, he launches a straight thrust attack, catching Thomas Corlette unawares. (Scottish Open men's individual foil semi-final, Edinburgh, 2014. Cook won 15/3.)

TALENT OR HARD WORK?

As Corlette (left) moves in at close quarters, Cook is already positioning his blade well behind his back, placing the hit at close quarters with apparent ease while Corlette looks on. (Scottish Open men's individual foil semi-final, Edinburgh, 2014.)

TALENT OR HARD WORK?

A sudden burst of speed by Zsolt Nagy (right) catches Michael Clarke temporarily off guard, as Clarke rapidly retreats… too late. (Scottish Open men's individual sabre semi-final, Edinburgh, 2014. Nagy won 15/11.)

Catriona Sibert (left) fights Victoria Duxbury. Sibert's single-minded determination to place the point carefully on Duxbury's foil target is evident in this sequence. (Scottish Open women's individual foil semi-final, Edinburgh, 2014. Sibert won 15/4.)

Aspiring to High Performance

Is there such a thing as innate talent? The obvious answer seems to be 'yes'. But the closer psychologists look at the careers of the gifted, the smaller the role innate talent seems to play: the bigger role is preparation. (Gladwell, 2008)

Coyle (2010, p.49) claims that, rather than our brains being fixed at birth, '…research has revealed that they are capable of building new and vastly improved circuitry through a combination of intensive practice and motivation. This connection is summarized in the "Rule of 10,000 Hours" – the amount of time performers in all domains… have been found to practise intensively to reach world-class status.' However, Winner (2010, p.49) suggests two flaws in the denial of inborn talent or intellectual potential: 'First, the fact that no one achieves at élite levels without significant effort shows that hard work is necessary, not that it is sufficient. In addition, the reverse is also likely: innate talent may be a necessary condition for hard work.'

In asking if winners possess innate traits from birth or should the development of talent be considered more important, Whyte (2012) writes: 'Despite the certain influences of genes on performance, their importance is often overstated. One irrefutable fact exists within the nature versus nurture debate: training is a critical element of the nurture algorithm, a key plank in the optimizing of physical, psychological and technical performance. But training is not everything. A complex bio-social interaction exists including factors such as family, coaching, facilities, wealth, sports structure, sport science and medicine…' In fact, scientists are learning that we have more capacity for lifelong learning and brain development than was previously realized. (Dweck, 2007, p.5)

Most people play sports or pursue interests well enough to enjoy them, but few are great. Great performers seem to be able to do effortlessly certain things that most of us cannot imagine doing. We assume outstanding performers must possess staggering intelligence or gigantic memories: some do, but many do not. (Colvin, 2010) Also, excellence on its own is not sufficient for success. Top sportspeople often exhibit an extraordinary ability to rise above the anxieties and angst, the doubts and tensions, that often paralyse lesser performers. They retain all those deep complex motor skills built up over thousands of hours of practice. (Syed, 2010) It has also been suggested that: 'With practice, training, and above all, method, we manage to increase our attention, our memory, our judgement and literally become more intelligent than we were before.' (Binet, 1975, cited in Dweck, 2007, p.5)

In studying the process of learning complex motor skills, it has been suggested that: 'Recent research investigating the influence of initial practice with the dominant vs. non-dominant hand on the acquisition of new throwing skills suggests complex motor skills that place high demands on the processing of visuo-spatial information are better learned after initial practice with the non-dominant hand.' (Stöckel and Weigelt, 2012 cited in Esteves, et al., 2015, p18) Of particular relevance to fencing is the finding that practising with the non-dominant hand improves performance on the dominant side.

Rule of 10,000 Hours

The more experience we have with something, the stronger the memory, or learning trace, for that experience becomes. (Levitin, 2006)

In a study in the early 1900s, the psychologist K. Anders Ericsson and two colleagues at Berlin's élite Academy of Music, with the help of the academy's professors, divided the

TALENT OR HARD WORK?

80

TALENT OR HARD WORK?

ABOVE AND OPPOSITE: Fighting back from a 'down' position is characteristic of many a high-performance fencer. Here, Catriona Sibert (left) takes an early lead but Lisa McKenzie fights doggedly back to win. (Scottish Open women's individual foil final, Edinburgh, 2014.)

81

TALENT OR HARD WORK?

Keith Cook (right) crouches momentarily before launching a sudden flèche attack on Patrick Daley. (Scottish Open men's individual foil final, Edinburgh, 2014. Cook won 15/6.)

TALENT OR HARD WORK?

Zsolt Nagy (right) scores a lightning fast stop-cut against (his brother) Pál Nagy, while approaching perilously close to the rear line of the piste. A fraction of a second after the hit lands, Zsolt leaves the piste. The hit is correctly awarded in Zsolt's favour. (Scottish Open men's individual sabre final, Edinburgh, 2014. Zsolt Nagy won 15/11.)

school's violinists into three groups. The first group were the 'stars', the students with the potential to become world-class soloists. In the second were those judged merely to be 'good'. In the third were students who were unlikely to ever play professionally. All the violinists were asked the same question: over the course of your entire career, ever since you first picked up the violin, how many hours have you practised? Everyone from all three groups started playing at roughly the same age, about five years old.

In the first few years, the practice record was similar for all, about two to three hours a week. But when the students were about eight years old, real differences started to emerge. The students who would end up the best in their class would practise more than everyone else: typically six hours a week by age nine, eight hours a week by age twelve, sixteen hours a week by age fourteen, and so on; until by age twenty they were practising well over thirty hours a week. In fact, by age twenty, the élite performers had each totalled 10,000 hours of practice. Interestingly, in the same study, they were unable to find any 'naturals': people who floated to the top effortlessly while practising for a fraction

83

of the time that the others did. Nor could they find any people who worked harder than anyone else, yet did not have what it takes to get to the top. Their research suggested that once a musician had enough ability to get into a top music school, the thing that distinguished one performer from another was how hard they worked. People at the very top worked much harder. (Gladwell, 2008, pp.38–40)

Levitin (2006, p.197) writes that: 'The emerging picture from such studies is that 10,000 hours of practice is required to achieve the level of mastery associated with being a world-class expert – in anything. In study after study… this number comes up again and again. 10,000 hours is equivalent to roughly three hours a day, or twenty hours a week, of practice over ten years. Of course this doesn't address why some people don't seem to get anywhere when they practise, and why some people get more out of their practice sessions than others. But no one has yet found a case in which true world-class expertise was accomplished in less time. It seems that it takes the brain this long to assimilate all that it needs to know to achieve true mastery.'

Contemporary athletes are superior, not because they are particularly different in some way, but because they train themselves more effectively. It seems that the right kind of practice can turn someone of unremarkable endowments into a much better, even an exceptional performer. (Colvin, 2010, p9) Ericsson, Krampe and Tesch-Romer (1993, p.363) suggest that in most domains of expertise, individuals begin with a regime of effortful activities in their childhoods (also called 'deliberate practice') that are designed to optimize improvement. They further suggest that individual differences, even amongst élite performers, are related closely to the extent of deliberate practice undertaken. Many characteristics once believed to reflect innate talent are actually the result of intense practice, extended for a minimum of ten years.

Deliberate Practice

Colvin (2010, pp.7–8) notes that deliberate practice is a large concept, and to say that it explains everything would be simplistic and reductive. Critical questions present themselves immediately: What exactly needs to be practised and how? Which specific skills or other assets must be acquired? The chief constraint seems to be mental, even in sports where physical demands seem the hardest.

Deliberate practice is hard, it hurts, but it works. It is designed to improve performance but without an unbiased view of the subject's performance, choosing the best practice activity is near to impossible. Deliberate practice requires that one identifies certain sharply defined elements of performance that need improvement, and then work on them intently. Choosing these aspects of performance is in itself an important skill and these aspects have to be repeated a lot. So getting feedback from a teacher, coach or mentor is crucial. All this places enormous strain on an athlete's mental abilities. Deliberate practice demands that instead of doing what we are good at, we seek out insistently what we are not good at. We identify painful, difficult activities that will make us better and do those things repeatedly. After each repetition we force ourselves to see, or get others to tell us, exactly what is still not right, so we can repeat the most difficult parts of what we have just done and continue that process until mentally exhausted. (Colvin, 2010)

Practice in great performers takes them around the limitations most of us think of as critical. Specifically, it enables them to perceive more, to know more and to remember more than most others do. Many years of intensive deliberate practice actually change the body and the brain. Sometimes great performers see more by developing a better and faster understanding of what they see. This superior perception extends beyond the sense of sight. They hear more when they listen and feel more when they touch. They also understand the significance of indicators that average performers do not notice. (Colvin, 2010)

'A finding that is remarkably consistent across disciplines is that four or five hours a day seems to be the upper limit of deliberate practice, and this is frequently accomplished in sessions lasting no more than an hour to ninety minutes.' (Colvin, 2010, p.71)

Next, we will explore how the belief that your abilities can be developed can lead to improved performance.

Mindset

An educational psychologist called Carol Dweck found the key to achieving your potential is not ability or talent, but your belief about ability. You either believe that abilities are natural and need to be demonstrated or that abilities can be developed. What she identified as 'mindset' is really a belief in what the sporting world refers to as talent. She went on to identify two types of mindset: fixed and growth. Someone with a tendency towards a fixed mindset believes their abilities are natural; they have certain abilities which cannot be changed. Someone with a tendency towards a growth mindset believes their abilities can be developed through learning and hard work; here, failures are seen as learning opportunities. (Sportscotland. n.d.)

Some of the differences in behaviour that you might recognize in more fixed and growth athletes and coaches are shown in the panel entitled Fixed and Growth Mindsets.

Fixed and Growth Mindsets

	Fixed Mindset	**Growth Mindset**
Leads to…	…a desire to show off talent and therefore a tendency to…	…a desire to learn and therefore a tendency to…
Challenges	…avoid challenges	…embrace challenges
Setbacks	…give up easily	…persist in the face of setbacks
Effort	…see effort as fruitless or worse	…see effort as the path to mastery
Criticism	…ignore useful negative feedback	…learn from criticism
Failure	…reflects a lack of talent	…is a learning opportunity
Potential	…is measured by current performance (e.g. personal best or current skills)	…cannot be measured
Success of others	…feel threatened by the success of others	…find lessons and inspiration from the success of others
As a result…	May plateau early and 'underachieve'	Reach ever higher levels of achievement

(Sportscotland, n.d., p.2)

TALENT OR HARD WORK?

Four Types of Behaviours

Challenges	Do you embrace *or* avoid them?
Setbacks	Do you persist when things go wrong *or* go back and focus on what you can do?
Criticism	Accept and learn from it *or* ignore it?
Ownership	I am responsible *or* my coach/manager is responsible?

(Sportscotland, n.d., p.5)

Dweck (2007, p.11) found those with a fixed mindset tended to have inaccurate ideas about their performance and ability, while those with a growth mindset were remarkably accurate. You need accurate information about your abilities in order to learn effectively.

Mindset is linked to what you achieve and explains why some athletes (apparently) go beyond their potential. They continue to work out how to improve. If you approach sport with a growth mindset you are likely to be more focused and train hard. (Sportscotland. n.d.) Four mindset behaviours have been suggested as being particularly relevant in sport, which are shown in the panel entitled Four Types of Behaviours.

Growth Mindset

People with a growth mindset find success in doing their best, in learning and improving: the typical behaviour of champions. Setbacks are motivating and informative. Such people take charge of the processes that bring and maintain success. People in a growth mindset do not just seek challenges, they thrive on them. (Dweck, 2007) Furthermore, it has been suggested that exceptional individuals have 'a special talent for identifying their own strengths and weaknesses.' (Gardiner, 1997 cited in Dweck, 2007, p.11)

There is a popular belief with children that praise can have beneficial effects on motivation. However, studies have shown that well-meant praise for intelligence, intended to boost children's enjoyment, persistence and performance during achievement, does not prepare them for coping with setbacks. It is better to separate the 'deed from the doer', by applying praise to children's strategies and work habits, rather than any particular trait. Since children cannot be insulated from failure throughout their lives, great care should be taken to send motivationally beneficial messages after successful outcomes. (Mueller and Dweck, 1998, pp.33–52)

Dweck provides some advice to parents, teachers and coaches in the panel entitled Grow Your Mindset.

Changing Your Mindset

Your mindset affects how you think, which in turn affects what you do. Hence, to change your mindset you will need to change how you think and how this thinking is reflected in how you behave. If your coach asks you to learn a new routine that appears very complicated, if you have a fixed mindset you may doubt you have the inherent ability to learn this new task. However, if you change to a growth mindset you might think that, because it looks complicated, you are unlikely to learn it quickly. With your coach's help, you will get there. (Sportscotland. n.d.)

You always have choices about how to think. It is important to set realistic goals

TALENT OR HARD WORK?

> **GROW YOUR MINDSET (ABRIDGED)**
>
> - Every word and action from parent to child sends a message… Are they messages that say: *You have permanent traits and I'm judging them?* Or are they messages that say: *You're a developing person and I'm interested in your development?*
> - How do you use praise? Remember that praising children's intelligence or talent, tempting as it is, sends a fixed-mindset message. It makes their confidence and motivation more fragile. Instead, try to focus on the *processes* they used – their strategies, effort or choices…
> - …Remember that constructive criticism is feedback that helps the child understand how to fix something.
> - Parents often set goals their children can work towards. Remember that having innate talent is not a goal. Expanding skill and knowledge is…
> - If you're a teacher, remember that lowering standards doesn't raise students' self-esteem. But neither does raising standards without giving students ways of reaching them. The growth mindset gives you a way to set high standards and have students reach them. Try presenting topics in a growth framework and giving students process feedback…
> - …Remember that great teachers believe in the growth of talent and intellect…
> - Are you a fixed-mindset coach…intolerant of mistakes? …Try on the growth mindset… ask for full commitment and full effort…
> - As parents, teachers and coaches, our mission is developing people's potential…
>
> (Dweck, 2007, pp.211–212)

around what you want to achieve. Try to be really specific about the areas you choose and how some improvement might impact on your performance. Write it down and share it with your coach/mentor. Set a time limit for this change in behaviour, say about six weeks. At the end of this period, decide whether the change has been helpful or not, and use this information to set a new goal. Keep repeating this process indefinitely. (Sportscotland. n.d.)

Main Points

- Few fencers are great. Those that are great often exhibit extraordinary abilities. They retain complex motor skills built up over thousands of hours of practice. 10,000 hours of practice is the level of mastery associated with being a world-class expert.
- Deliberate practice is hard, it hurts, but it works. Sharply defined elements of performance, that need improvement, are worked on with many repetitions; this places an enormous strain on a fencer's mental abilities. Four to five hours a day seems to be the upper limit for deliberate practice, with sessions lasting no more than an hour to ninety minutes.
- Mindset is linked to what you achieve and explains why some athletes go beyond their potential. People with a growth mindset find success in doing their best, in learning and improving.
- Praise children for their strategies and work habits, rather than for any particular trait.

CHAPTER FIVE

SPORTS PSYCHOLOGY

Develop belief. Belief is the birth of excellence. You are what you believe. Beliefs are like commanders of the brain.

(Kogler, 2005, p.10)

Once again we see high-performance fencers in action.

In observing these athletes, it is important to understand that: 'Fencing is as much a mind game as a physical test. Even though you face one another through the mesh in the mask, your confrontation with opponents is eyeball to eyeball, with all the mental pressure this entails.' (Kingston, 2001, pp.62–63) As well as being physically fit, what makes their sharpness of action and reaction possible is the degree of mental fitness these combatants can muster.

Camden International Cadet Sabre, London, 2014. Paolo Guzzon of Italy, left, fights Great Britain's Christian Lindsay. Guzzon won 15/12. (Photo: Graham Morrison)

SPORTS PSYCHOLOGY

Mhairi de Sainte Croix (left) takes an early lead against Hannah Nesbitt and holds on to it. (Scottish Open women's individual épée semi-final, Edinburgh, 2014. de Sainte Croix won 15/5.)

SPORTS PSYCHOLOGY

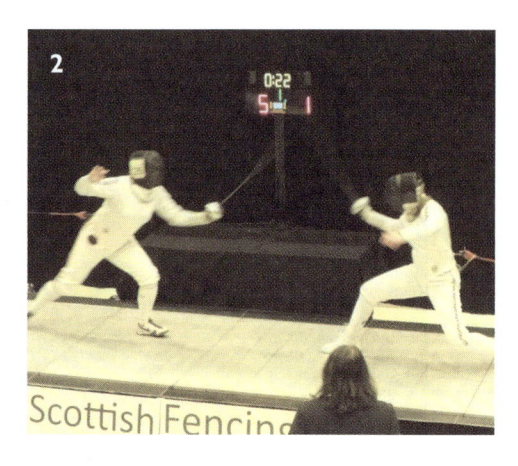

ABOVE AND OPPOSITE: *An attack consisting of five blade actions.*

SPORTS PSYCHOLOGY

SPORTS PSYCHOLOGY

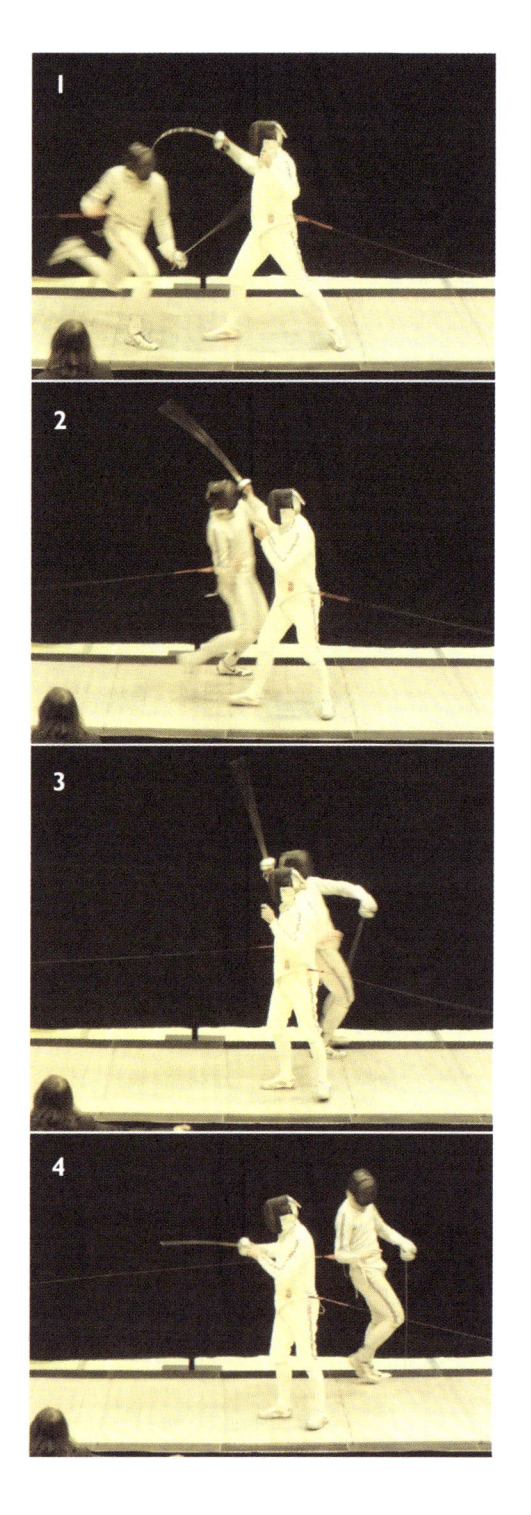

Calum Johnston (left) fights back against Anton Pollard and takes the lead. Note there is a riposte to leg. (Scottish Open men's individual épée semi-final, Edinburgh, 2014. Johnston won 15/11.)

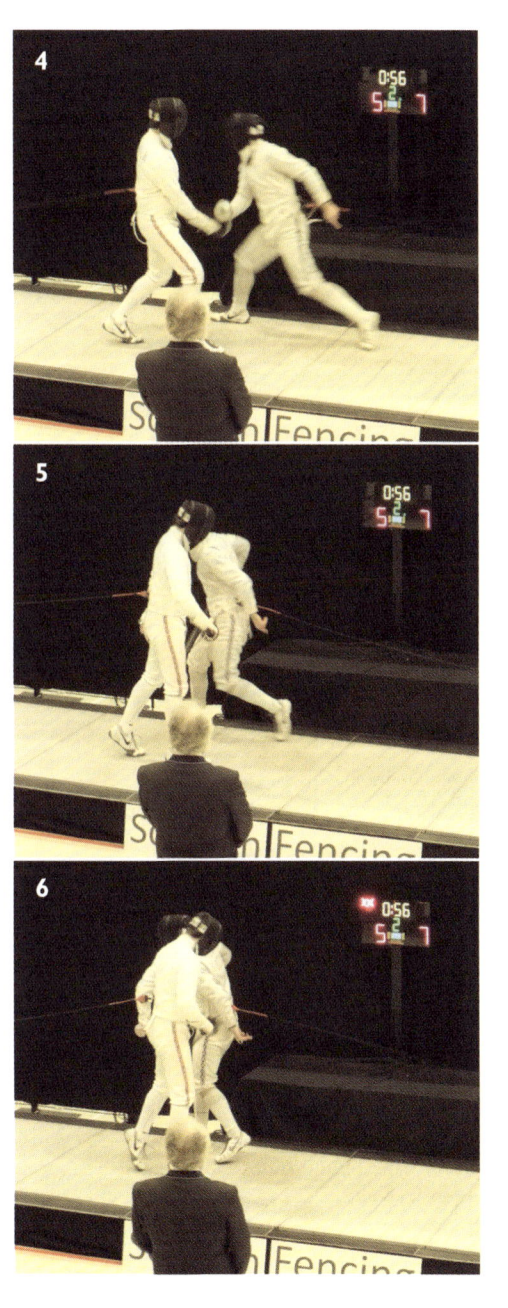

SPORTS PSYCHOLOGY

Neill Tannock (left) scores a hit at close quarters as Christopher Rocks moves in. (Scottish Open men's individual épée semi-final, Edinburgh, 2014. Rocks won 15/12.)

93

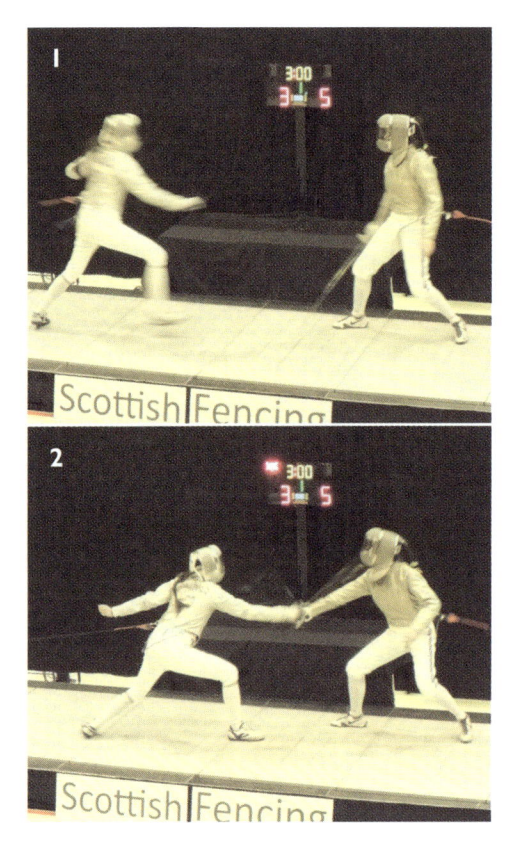

SPORTS PSYCHOLOGY

Sara Palings (left) scores with a fast attack on Sarah-Jane Hampson, and Sarah-Jane Hampson responds in similar vein. (Scottish Open women's individual sabre semi-final, Edinburgh, 2014 Hampson won 15/10.)

Psychological Preparation

Kogler (2005, p.7) writes that: 'Everything begins with your thinking processes. Your life is the result of your thoughts, so you must become very responsible and very, very careful about what you think – because what you think is going to manifest itself in reality... the moment you begin to evaluate your own thoughts, you will realize that you have a *choice* – to go with them or to *regulate* them... you can regulate your thought processes – by focusing on the thoughts you *want* to think.' Start by thinking of yourself as a serious athlete. (Paul, *et al.*, 2012, p.78)

Look at the panel entitled Consider the Following Words and What They Mean to You. Many of these qualities you will instantly recognize as belonging to someone who is destined for success. Next, look at the panel entitled Within Any Successful Person You Will Find... can you see yourself?

Alaux (1975, pp.182–183) makes some interesting points: 'Psychological preparation is necessary so that the fencer learns to relax

SPORTS PSYCHOLOGY

Calum Johnston (left) takes a high parry of sixte, riposting low against Christopher Rocks, resulting in a double hit. Scottish Open men's individual épée final, Edinburgh, 2014. Johnston won 15/14.)

Kate Daykin (left) leads as Sarah-Jane Hampson launches her attack. (Scottish Open women's individual sabre final, Edinburgh, 2014. Daykin won 15/6.)

CONSIDER THE FOLLOWING WORDS AND WHAT THEY MEAN TO YOU

- Motivation
- Commitment
- Determination
- Discipline
- Focus
- Self-belief
- Enthusiasm
- Knowledge
- Positive thinking
- Adaptability

(Cochrane, n.d., p.19)

WITHIN ANY SUCCESSFUL PERSON YOU WILL FIND…

- Utter determination, focus and drive to reach their goals.
- A continuous search for ways to improve.
- The motivation and focus to go on when things do not go to plan.
- The ability to remain positive and to learn from mistakes.
- An insatiable thirst for knowledge.
- Enthusiasm and belief that what they are doing with their life is right.

(Cochrane, n.d., p.19)

SPORTS PSYCHOLOGY

under pressure and to concentrate his (/her) energies to achieve explosive reactions.

'Let us consider two individuals who may maintain the same posture but differ in the following respect: Where one has relaxed muscles on both sides of a joint, the other has tensed muscles. The one who has both sets of muscle relaxed merely has to tighten one set to produce the desired movement. The one who has both sets tensed must first relax the opposing muscles before the desired movement can be started. This leads to a loss of speed and a jerkiness or irregularity in the movement. To summarize, in combat, the ultimate aim of conditioning is to achieve mobility and crisp actions *without prior tense muscles*.'

The aim here is to achieve a form of relaxed tension, where the individual is prepared to move but is physically not tense in any way: the tension is mental.

'Fencing is a combative sport. The will power and intelligence of the opponent have to be reckoned with in it.' (Beke and Polgár, 1963, p.29) It follows, therefore, that a better understanding of the different types of fencers should help us compete more effectively.

Types of Fencers

Knowledge of the more common personality types in fencing will help in selecting which tactics should be employed and in understanding how our own personalities operate when we fence.

Active and passive fencer types represent opposite extremes. An active fencer attempts to impose his/her will on the opponent, perhaps launching offensive actions early on. He/she generally displays a preference for offensive, rather than defensive actions and is highly motivated, with a strong desire to win. On the other hand, he/she may lack self-control, lack careful planning and not understand tactical situations properly. A passive fencer tends to leave the initiative up to the opponent, favours defensive actions and prefers careful manoeuvring on the piste, waiting patiently for a chance to hit. He or she prefers to wait until the opponent makes mistakes, rather than create tactical situations. He/she may often delay decisions, missing good opportunities to score a hit. (Czajkowski, 2005, pp.158–60)

Fencers of foreseen and improvised actions tend to be at opposite extremes. A fencer of foreseen actions likes premeditation and carefully observes the opponent, trying to seize an opportunity to use a previously thought-out action. On the other hand, a fencer of foreseen actions may lose out on scoring a hit on the spur of the moment, and may have a predilection for first, or second intention, or both. A fencer who improvises does so without any preconceived plan of action. He/she uses a variety of actions, is able to make lightning decisions and has great speed and accuracy of perception. On the other hand, he/she may be unable to penetrate the thoughts and intentions of the opponent, lack observational skills and miss chances through not spotting obvious weaknesses. (Czajkowski, 2005, pp.160–162)

Fencers of cooperative and contradictory tactics are opposite extremes. One who cooperates, tends to use long phrases, reacts initially in apparent compliance with the opponent's intentions, but finishes with an extra movement, unforeseen by the opponent. Two examples of cooperative tactics follow:

(1) 'The fencer foresees the opponent's compound attack consisting of two feints and the final stroke. He (/she) reacts to

the feints by successive parries – which are what the opponent expected – then unexpectedly adds still another parry and scores a hit with the riposte.'

(2) 'The opponent repeats several times, in succession, a quarte pressure on the blade. The fencer realizes that the opponent wants to draw his (/her) attack by double disengagement in order to parry the attack and hit with the riposte. Therefore he (/she) executes the opponent's desired attack as a false attack with a rather short lunge, then parries the opponent's riposte and scores a hit with a counter-riposte (thus executing one variety of second-intention attack). This is, of course, a sometimes rather risky form of tactics – one may not rightly guess the opponent's real intentions – but it is very often successful at leading the opponent into a trap.'

One who contradicts uses simple, short phrases and, having understood the opponent's intentions, then applies at once some uncomplicated fast action that spoils the opponent's plans. Two examples of contradictory tactics follow:

(1) 'Against an expected attack with feints, the fencer of contradictory tactics will not react by parries but will execute a stop-hit or a stop-hit with opposition.'

(2) 'A foilist, having guessed that his (/her) opponent wants to provoke him (/her) into making an attack by double disengagement, will not comply with his (/her) wishes but will instantly disengage and execute a counter-sixte beat followed by a straight thrust.'
(Czajkowski, 2005, pp.162–164)

We can also distinguish between fencers with a wide range and others with a narrow range of actions. A fencer with a wide range will apply offensive, defensive and counter-offensive actions with great variety and cleverness. The opposite is the fencer who always uses the same limited range of actions in a bout. His/her strong points are extreme confidence, accompanied by technical expertise at performing his/her limited repertoire. (Czajkowski, 2005, pp.164–165)

Some fencers are cautious and others risk-takers. A cautious fencer exhibits a very high level of concentration and is careful not to take any risks, waiting for a sure opportunity to score a hit. A risk-taker does not concentrate enough, may score hits by being bold but often receives easy hits against through lack of careful observation. (Czajkowski, 2005, p.165)

Fencers may also display offensive or defensive extremes. The offensive fencer relies mainly on real or false attacks. The defensive fencer is more cautious, relying mainly on defensive or counter-offensive actions. (Czajkowski, 2005, pp.165–166)

The better we understand ourselves and others' motivations when we fence, the more we are able to prepare ourselves for the psychological challenges that lie ahead.

Psychological Challenges

Kogler (2005, p.102) writes that: 'Studies show that successful fencers *send themselves very different mental messages than fencers who are less successful.* Successful fencers concentrate on the process of fencing (the bout). Unsuccessful fencers are overwhelmed by frustration and negative thoughts about their mistakes.'

A list of qualities typically found in a successful fencer can be read in the panel entitled Within Any Successful Person You Will Find.

SPORTS PSYCHOLOGY

> **WITHIN ANY SUCCESSFUL PERSON YOU WILL FIND**
>
> - Utter determination, focus and drive to reach their goals.
> - A continuous search for ways to improve.
> - The motivation and focus to go on when things do not go to plan.
> - The ability to remain positive and to learn from mistakes.
> - An insatiable thirst for knowledge.
> - Enthusiasm and belief that what they are doing with their life is right.
>
> (Cochrane, n.d., p.19)

The psychological challenges inherent in the process of getting to the top in fencing are listed in the panel entitled Psychological Difficulties.

Motivation and Arousal

All fencing activities are influenced by an immense number of factors, among which are motivation and arousal. Motivation includes factors such as ambition, the desire to achieve and to fulfil a need. It influences our behaviours, activities and attitudes. Motivation is a psychological process. Arousal is a physiological process. In the majority of cases, with an increase of motivation comes an increase in the level of arousal. (Czajkowski, 2005, pp.109–111)

Wlodzimierz Szewczuk (cited in Czajkowski, 2005, p.108) writes: 'Motivation does not bring results unless a person realizes the aim of the activity and the practical means of achieving the goal.' Richard H. Cox (cited in Czajkowski, 2005, p.109) suggests that: 'To understand arousal is to understand what basic changes take place in the body when the organism is activated. When we speak of arousal, we are talking about the degree of activation of the organs that are under the control of the autonomic nervous system.'

Extroverts differ from introverts when it comes to achieving optimum arousal. Extroverts tend to be stimulus-hungry, very lively, very active, talkative, noisy and fond of change. Introverts try to avoid stimuli, are not very talkative, not particularly lively and avoid noisy company, in order to preserve their optimal levels of arousal. (Czajkowski, 2005, p.110)

> **PSYCHOLOGICAL DIFFICULTIES**
>
> 1. The life-changing significance of (not) winning high-profile events.
> 2. The constant need to strategize tactics and training to fend off the competition.
> 3. The relentless, intense training needed to develop your capabilities to a world-class level.
> 4. The setbacks of injury recovery, which could be as much as six months or even more.
> 5. Finding financial support while you train and compete full-time.
> 6. The unfamiliar international competition environment, foreign languages, practices and so on.
> 7. The intense competitive national selection process at home: typically you need to keep in the top ten to fifteen rankings to be able to represent the country, and very near the top to be automatically selected as part of the national team.
>
> (Paul, et al., 2012, p.136)

SPORTS PSYCHOLOGY

You will not fence well if your levels of arousal and anxiety are low. On the other hand, once you exceed a certain level of arousal and anxiety, your ability to fence will taper off quickly. You need to be able to recognize when you are in the zone that is good for you. High arousal in an élite athlete can be beneficial, so long as anxiety is kept under control. (Paul, et al., 2012, p.79)

As Kogler points out (2005, p.45): 'Control of arousal is a critical factor in competition. Performance anxiety is a negative heightened state of arousal... If you are experiencing high anxiety, direct and maintain your focus exclusively on the task in hand. Stop focusing on extraneous external factors like the crowd, your teammates, etc; stop focusing inward on your doubts.'

A fencer with optimal arousal perceives only relevant stimuli. A fencer with too high a level of arousal does not perceive, or perceives too late, relevant stimuli, that can lead to defeat. (Czajkowski, 2005, p.127)

It is possible to differentiate between intrinsic and extrinsic motivation. Intrinsic motivation means that we want to do something because it is satisfying, gives us pleasure and we think it is good for us. Extrinsic motivation means that we do something, not so much for its own sake, but because we have to, or perhaps expect some gain, that will provide us with a degree of satisfaction. Usually, the effects of intrinsic motivation are positive. We end up doing things much better. Intrinsic motivation diminishes the perception of fatigue, helps the process of recovery and leads to a high levels of interest in one's sport. (Czajkowski, 2005, pp.112-113) The salient features of intrinsic motivation are summarized in the panel entitled Intrinsic Motivation.

The strength of the nervous system determines the quality of motor performance – including those in sport activities – indirectly,

INTRINSIC MOTIVATION

- Activity (exercise, competitions and everything connected with fencing) that is influenced by intrinsic motivation form a source of pleasure, joy and satisfaction.
- One does, efficiently and eagerly, what one likes and what gives one pleasure.
- Intrinsic motivation encourages activity; it is conducive to a deep and many-sided analysis of our possibilities, training, results in competitions, etc, and gives insight to new and more efficient ways of solving the problems connected with cultivating fencing.

(Czajkowski, 2005, p.113)

-through motivation. (V.A. Vyatkin cited in Czajkowski, 2005, p.126) Thus, during practice, athletes with a weak nervous system often show a high level of performance, but in competition their level of performance is much lower and inconsistent. Strong types act efficiently in difficult situations and their results in competitions tend to be higher than during practice. (Czajkowski, 2005, p.126) Physical fitness is also necessary. Barbara Knapp (cited in Czajkowski, 2005, pp.132-133) expresses the view that: 'It is highly unlikely that a person could achieve significant results in a given game or sport, if his or her motivation did not include the need of perfecting his or her own physical fitness, as an aim in itself.'

Executing difficult actions under pressure can often be problematic. One way of overcoming this is by using the over-learning method, which was introduced in the first half of the nineteenth century by the French master Jean Louis de Montpellier (cited in

SPORTS PSYCHOLOGY

PRACTICAL GUIDELINES

- *Strengthen* your intuition. Though intuition is not a conscious process, you can take conscious steps to strengthen it.
- *Listen* to the signals your mind sends to your body. Train yourself to pay attention to what your intuition is telling you…
- *Listen* to your mind and to your body. Make a conscious effort to attune yourself to the fleeting feelings of intuition. Always keep an open mind and suspend judgement…
- Cultivate *careful observation*. Pay attention to details. Look for what is out of sync or out of balance.
- *Watch DVDs* of your bouts; analyse them carefully from all aspects: techniques, tactics, your emotion and thoughts.
- *Watch your opponents* when they fence against other fencers: what tactics and what strokes do they use against them? Watch the top fencers carefully. Keep a 'library' about your opponents, about their bouts and action.
- *Write down* your observations and experiences. Writing them down is better than just thinking about them…
- *Feed* your intuition. Intuition is only as powerful as the 'library' of prior experiences it can call up.
- *Develop* your intuition. Gather a wide range of different experiences in fencing. Experience is required for expertise in every profession. If you want to be a top fencer, you must fence. Fence, bout, compete against a variety of fencers with different styles, tactics and skill levels under varied conditions and in diverse situations. Seek deep, broad experience.
- Always *fence with full concentration*. Immerse yourself in the bout situations. You cannot recognize any patterns until you have spent enough time and paid enough attention to a situation to get beneath the surface.
- *Fence against a variety of opponents*. It is not enough to fence only against élite fencers and to prepare for their style, tactics, etc.
- *Fully absorb and process* what you experience. Record your experiences in your personal diary. You will get into more depth and detail about your experiences and observations, and thus you will understand them more fully.
- *Keep a journal* to bring your intuitive power to the surface. Write consciously about what you want to understand more deeply. This exercise forces you to probe into the meaning of details and to see patterns you missed while you were experiencing the events.
- *Learn from other fencers*, especially the ones who have excellent judgement. Learn from older, experienced teammates. Profit from their experience. You can learn from them just by watching them closely…
- *Spend as much time as possible* around élite, experienced smart fencers with great intuition.
- *Harness the power of teamwork*. Three hard-working fencers with their own experiences and distinct points of view can see far more patterns than can one individual – even a brilliant one. When a team truly bonds, exciting things happen through the synergy of joint intuition. You will come away from the process with invaluable additions to your mind's database.
- *Invest time in your intuition*. It takes literally thousands of hours to truly develop your intuition in fencing.

(Kogler, 2005, pp.39–42)

SPORTS PSYCHOLOGY

Czajkowski, 2005, pp.130-131). This consists of becoming accustomed to using difficult movements and sequences in complicated, changeable conditions for long periods of time. This will have the effect that simpler strokes, subsequently used in exacting conditions, will subjectively appear less daunting.

Intuition

Kogler (2005, p.38) writes that: 'Intuition can be generally defined as the mind's ability to match patterns. The fencer "gets a feeling" about a new situation because it is subconsciously similar to an experience he (/she) has had before. In épée fencing, intuition tells us

---

DEVELOPING SELF-CONFIDENCE

- Physically staying in shape will help you psychologically. The more you practise, the better you should feel...
- Increase your self-discipline. Years of hard, disciplined practice give you the satisfying knowledge of being in total control of yourself...
- Work on improving your fencing technique and tactics. Fencing makes higher demands on technique than any other sport.
- In training, always focus on your weaknesses. Write down the thing you plan to work on to help improve your technique and to eliminate weaknesses. By increasing your fencing-specific fitness and your technique you will increase the feeling and knowledge of being in control, which in turn increases your self-confidence.
- Practise and practise, drill and drill, so that your body reacts automatically and you gain confidence.
- Give your (training) partner an advantage, compete with handicaps such as starting out behind by two touches or not being allowed to use your strongest actions.
- Compete in more tournaments – weaker ones if necessary – to experience winning under pressure.
- Set realistic goals for yourself. You can't control the final outcome, only the process. Winning will take care of itself...
- Use positive self-talk. Think, imagine and say positive thoughts to increase self-confidence...
- Simulate your important bout or competition. In the last phase before your target (most important) competition... take part in a simulated event... At the end, note all the positive elements that you achieved as well as your weak points that need to be worked on further.
- Watch your pre-competition music DVD. The evening before your competition, watch a music DVD of your best bout (competition) with well-chosen music...
- As you watch, recapture all the positive feelings and thoughts that accompanied these best bouts. See, hear and feel everything that happened. Regain this winning feeling, the sense of being on top of your game, unbeatable.
- Fence with detachment, effortlessly – one touch, one bout at a time. Do not worry about your performance, problems, past and future. It will lead to anxiety and helpless feelings.
- Focus on the here and now.

(Kogler, 2005, pp.58–60)

SPORTS PSYCHOLOGY

to go ahead and *repeat the same foot-touch a third time,* and intuition tells an experienced master to choose to work with one "future champion" among many aspiring students.' Intuition works subconsciously. It integrates how you feel with how you think, in order to reach a conclusion. It is only after that you become aware of intuitive feelings that logical intelligence comes into play.

A list of practical guidelines about intuition are included in the panel of the same name.

Self-Confidence

Consistent self-confidence means believing in your ability to cope with the challenges ahead. Many fencers do not believe in themselves. Often, the difference between success and failure is simply in the mind of the achiever. If you are insecure, others will sense it. Your perceptions about yourself and your opponent can have an immediate effect on how well you fence. Never think about failure or create imaginary obstacles in your mind. Confident, self-assured fencers generally feel very loose, very relaxed and are difficult to intimidate. They imagine themselves performing well. Confidence starts with your thoughts and feelings and works its way out into your fencing. It is a transient state. When performing wisely, it is easy to think confident thoughts but top athletes are able to separate themselves from the crowd and think confidently, even when performing poorly. Your thoughts are your own choices and responsibility, and you must choose them wisely. Progress can only come through positive, constructive thinking. Work hard to improve your physical condition. Train with maximum effort and make the most of every practice session. If you have prepared yourself physically and mentally and believe in your training programme, you will feel much more confident before a competition. (Kogler, 2005, pp.56–57)

To help develop self-confidence and achieve your goals, focus on the factors listed in the panel entitled Developing Self-Confidence.

Research into the confidence of élite athletes has suggests a number of areas that build and sustain sports confidence. These are itemised in the panel entitled Nine Areas That Build and Sustain Sports Confidence.

NINE AREAS THAT BUILD AND SUSTAIN SPORTS CONFIDENCE

1) Preparation – high-quality training and tactics analysis prior to competition.
2) Prior performance accomplishments.
3) Coaching – good-quality support and advice.
4) Social support – club, friends and family.
5) Innate factors – natural trait confidence.
6) Experience – familiarity with the competition and competitors, in dealing with setbacks and so on.
7) Competitive advantage – knowing you are better than your rivals, for example.
8) Trust – in yourself, your coach, teammates and organizing body.
9) Self-awareness – emotional control on and off the piste, and not making mistakes or gaffes that undermine your self-esteem.

(Bakker, *et al.*, 2011 cited in Paul, *et al.*, 2012, p.149)

SPORTS PSYCHOLOGY

Of these, the main source of confidence to world class athletes was found to be 1), 2) and 3). (Bakker, *et al.*, 2011 cited in Paul, *et al.*, 2012, p.149) Self-confidence to see through your tactic despite all the difficulties is particularly crucial. (Paul, *et al.*, 2012, p.136)

'Remember, confidence is mostly a state of mind and, while it takes effort, you can take control of how you perceive yourself and your world. More than that, your mental training can motivate you to go much, much further than you ever dreamt of.' (Paul, *et al.*, 2012, p. 149)

Relaxation by Breathing

By controlling and slowing down the rate of breathing, tension can be reduced, thereby increasing relaxation. (Brown and Adamson, 1995) Breathing is the only involuntary function that can be easily controlled. By changing our breathing, we change our mental state. Some athletes over-breathe (hyperventilate) when anxious or under stress; others actually 'forget' to breathe, holding their breath or breathing shallowly and infrequently when the pressure is on. The consequence is a chemical imbalance in the brain, which results in a state of stress. The close interplay of body, breath and consciousness is the basis of the use of breath to control the emotions. (Kogler, 2005, p.112–113)

Centring is a simple breathing technique. Try inhaling through your nose, with a slow, deep breath, expanding your navel area; then, exhale deeply through your mouth as the navel area contracts. Imagine that as you exhale, you are releasing all negative thoughts and tensions. While you are centring and thinking about centring, you cannot think negative thoughts. (Kogler, 2005, p.103)

This exercise in the panel entitled Centring,

CENTRING

- Sit alone in a quiet place.
- Sit comfortably. Close your eyes.
- Focus on your breathing, Concentrate on (visualize) the place where the air enters and leaves your nostrils as you inhale and exhale, or focus on the area of your stomach as it expand and contracts.
- After a minute or two, become aware of the sensations in your body, such as heaviness, and warmth.
- After a minute, bring your attention to the centre of your chest and lightly rest there. Thoughts and images will distract your attention. Do not resist or fight them but when you notice them, *gently* return your focus to your chest.
- Finish centring by doing nothing. Just sit quietly for a while. The negative energies have discharged. You will feel calm and light inside.

(Kogler, 2005, p.123)

which will take about three to five minutes, will help you become centred before a fencing competition.

Self-Talk and Imagery

Élite sportspeople use self-talks to realign their emotions, which is one way of replacing negative thinking. You can use self-talk, which is essentially those things that you say to yourself mentally, to fill your mind with positive sensations, to crowd out negative thoughts and to pre-programme your emotional state. (Paul, *et al.*, 2012, pp.81, 138)

To get the most out of imagery it is necessary to imagine a scene as perfectly as possi-

SPORTS PSYCHOLOGY

Eden Cup Junior 'A' Grade men's individual foil semi-final, London, 2013. Francesco Ingargiola of Italy talks to his coach Matteo Zennaro during the break. (Photo: Graham Morrison)

ble, ideally visualizing events as they happen through your own eyes. Skills-based imagery can be used to hardwire coaching and other learning. (Paul, et al., 2012, p.143) This is particularly useful if using your coach's training advice and observations from competitions as a basis for correction. Having your coach on hand at a fencing competition can of course be very useful. Not only can he/she observe you fencing but they are available during breaks to give helpful advice, as in the case of Francesco Ingargiola (ITA) and his coach Matteo Zennaro (at the Eden Cup, Men's Individual Foil). This was particularly so as Zennaro was able to draw on his own considerable personal experiences as a previous winner of the same competition.

Eden Cup Junior 'A' Grade men's individual foil, London, 2013. Italy's Matteo Zennaro, a previous winner of this event, was present as a coach. (Photo: Graham Morrison)

104

SPORTS PSYCHOLOGY

Eden Cup men's individual foil, London, 2013. Left-to-right. Maximilien Chastanet, France – silver; Francesco Ingargiola, Italy – gold; Thomas Antoine, France – bronze; Jerry Chang, USA – bronze. (Photo: Graham Morrison)

Having your own mantra, or set of mantras for different situations, will help overcome nerves and allow you to fence better. (Paul, et al., 2012, p.82) Harmenberg, et al., (2007, p.146) refer to a strategy of mental preparation before a match, where the following mantra would be repeated again and again in order to reach the right mental attitude: 'My opponent is better than I am but I will fight as hard as I can and make it as difficult as possible for him to win.' Although thinking this mantra was sufficient in most cases, thinking nothing was even better. Paul, et al., (2012, p.82) writes that: 'Harmenberg's state of mind where he thinks of nothing… frees up the faster, smarter subconscious, trusting it to fight to its best possible ability.'

When we dig into the minds of top sportspeople and explore the relationship between mind and body under pressure, we arrive at the paradoxical conclusion that the thing that often separates the best from the rest is a capacity to believe things that are not true but which are incredibly effective. (Syed, 2010, p.144) When we daydream, our minds wander and we visualize things. We are using imagery, the basic mental tool of visualization. (Kogler, 2005, p.214) Einstein (cited in Kogler,

SPORTS PSYCHOLOGY

2005, p.214) said: 'Imagery is more important than knowledge. I value more the gift of fantasy, than my ability to absorb positive knowledge.'

Mental imagery is an important part of thinking in our daily lives and is likely to play an important role in fencing. Mental imagery and perception share many functional and biological processes and its practice is likely to recruit the same neural pathways as actual fencing. (Esteves, et al., 2015, p.18)

The uses of mental imagery are set out in the panel entitled Five Types of Performance Enhancement.

'Imagery is an important tool for improving your performance and achieving self-control. The European term for this type of imagery utilization in sport is called ideomotor training (IT)' (Kogler, 2005, p.215) Try practising the following exercise a few days before a competition, to re-experience feelings of victory and inner safety. This is shown in the panel entitled IT for Recalling 'Winning Feelings' and Strengthening Confidence.

FIVE TYPES OF PERFORMANCE ENHANCEMENT

1) To hardwire fencing skills
2) Embedded strategies for fencing situations or dealing with particular opponent, or correcting bad habits…
3) For improving motivation…
4) Getting the right level of excitement/calm before and during competitions…
5) Improving your general self-confidence…

(Paul, et al., 2012, pp.81-82)

IT FOR RECALLING 'WINNING FEELINGS' AND STRENGTHENING CONFIDENCE

Recall one of your most successful bouts. Mentally re-experience it as vividly as possible… Use all your senses. Visualize yourself perfectly executing your performance; see and feel what you felt when you experienced the 'winning feeling'… Capture the fabulous feeling of victory; enjoy all over again the sense of success, confidence and accomplishment. Re-experience the feeling of inner safety.

Re-experiencing such feelings will strengthen your confidence, increase your belief in yourself and your ability, promote self-control and replace mental images from unsuccessful performances.

Bring your mind to the fencing hall where your next competition will take place. Then imagine fencing your best, being in your optimum state.

Make your imagery as sharp as possible, executing great actions, making great parry-ripostes, setting fantastic traps, attacks and counter-attacks – fencing like a superstar. Do not limit your expectations of success by making the imagery 'realistic'. Let your imagination go!

Finally bring the bout to an end.

Afterwards relax.

(Kogler, 2005, p.230)

SPORTS PSYCHOLOGY

Setting Goals

Michelangelo (cited in Kogler, 2005, p.214) suggested: 'The greater danger for most of us is not that we aim too high and miss our goal but that we aim too low and reach it.' Despite these cautionary words, one thing seems fairly clear: athletes who have goals tend to outperform their expectations. (Paul, et al., 2012, p.141)

Shepherd (2006, p.156-157) provides some useful advice on goal-setting when he writes: 'A very simple way of establishing a sports goal is to use the SMARTER (acronym) set of principles.

Specific. A goal must be focused and targeted…

Measurable. It is crucial for sports goals to be measurable… Objective training/competition goals must be established and measured by specifically designed workouts and tests to progress the athlete towards their main goal. Consequently, there should be main and sub-goals that are progressed through on the way to the main competitive goal. Again, these need to be objectively measurable.

Achievable. There is no point in setting an unattainable goal. Athlete/coach must consider training maturity, lifestyle, training options and facilities, and so on, in order to establish appropriate (and achievable) goals.

Realistic. Goals must fit the athlete's lifestyle and those whose lives are affected by the athlete, for example, partners and work colleagues. Training has to complement everyday life, not work against it. (It may be easier for full- or part-time athletes to achieve such a balance than those who work full-time and have family commitments…)

Targeted. It seems obvious that sports goals must be targeted… construct a relevant and progressive training plan with a designated time frame…

Empowering. Pursuing and achieving sports goals must be a positive process. The athlete (and the coach) must value what they are striving for…

Revisable… The goals of the athlete/coach must not be set in stone…

The basic assumption of goal-setting theory is that how well we perform tasks depends on the conscious goals we are trying for when we perform them. The general idea is that goals regulate human actions. It has been shown that specific, difficult, challenging goals lead to higher levels of performance. (Locke cited in Kogler, 2005, pp.98–99)

Two approaches to goal-setting and

TWO APPROACHES TO GOAL SETTING AND COMPETITION

1) Result focus or ego orientation
Athletes with result focus define success and failure in terms of winning and losing…

2) Action focus or task orientation
Athletes with this approach define success and failure in terms of personal mastery and self-improvement. For these athletes, satisfaction comes from achieving high goals consistently, from improvement and self-mastery. They focus on getting the work done. They don't worry about winning or losing or the praise or rewards they will receive. Their reward is the great satisfaction from improvement, self-mastery, and the enjoyment of the process itself.
(Locke cited in Kogler, 2005, pp.98–99)

SPORTS PSYCHOLOGY

competition are shown in the panel of the same name.

A study of Olympic athletes found that having multifaceted goals had a greater positive impact on their self-confidence than those who did not believe in goals. Their sporting performance was better too. (Connaughton, et al., 2008 cited in Paul, et al., 2012, p.141) Three types of basic goals are described in the panel entitled Goal Basics.

It is important to note that all of these goals focus on positive achievements. (Paul, et al., 2012, p.141)

Main Points

- What you think about manifests itself in reality. When you evaluate your own thoughts you begin to make choices.
- A better understanding of the different types of fencing personalities will help in understanding your opponent's and your own.
- Successful fencers concentrate on the processes of fencing, as discovered through bouts.
- Motivation is a psychological process. Arousal is a physiological process. Generally speaking, intuition is the mind's ability to match patterns. Intuition works subconsciously and integrates how you feel and think in order to reach a conclusion.
- If you prepare yourself physically and mentally, and believe in your training programme, you will feel more confident before a competition.
- Self-talk can be used to fill your mind with positive sensations, crowd out negative thoughts and pre-programme your emotional state.
- Imagery is an important tool for improving performance and achieving self-control. Skills-based imagery can be used to hard-wire coaching and other learning.
- Athletes with goals tend to exceed their expectations.

Goal Basics

Life Goals	…one, two or three vision statements that spell out what you want to do with your life, i.e. where do you want to be in five to ten years? … Your life goals have to have integrity: they have to be all about what you want to achieve and what you love doing…
Achievement Goals	…these are the stepping stones towards your life goals. They are measurable results you hope to achieve over the coming fencing season. They also have to be achievable and, in this way, have integrity. If your achievement goals are too ambitious… pressure and actual failure will dent your self-confidence… If they don't stretch you…they won't progress you towards your life goals. Your achievement dreams must be realistic plus twenty per cent but you should check them for realism with your coach. Your achievement goals may not refer to winning but to fencing at a very high standard. You know when you have fenced well, even when you have lost to a superior fencer… For fencing, achievement goals might involve getting to a certain point in the rankings or the quarter-finals at certain events…
Process Goals	…these goals are the measurable activities that help you to improve sufficiently to reach your achievement goals. These will typically include training goals but can also include other activities to facilitate your product goals…

(Paul, et al., 2012, p.141)

CHAPTER SIX

BECOMING A HIGH PERFORMANCE FENCER

A good fencer is like a good actor, who can play any role from comedy to drama.

(Lukovich, 2013, p.9)

Lukovich (2013, p.8) writes that: 'According to the classical definition, foil is the weapon of technique, sabre is the weapon of tactics, and épée is the weapon of tempo.' This is his view but other views also prevail. In all these disciplines, fencers communicate with each other through footwork and their use of weapons. They bring their own personal characteristics into play and seeing tends to be their primary means of gathering information. In the photographs that follow, fencers will warm up several times during the course of a competition and each does it in his or her own way. If a coach warms up a fencer

Assorted photographs from the Eden Cup Junior 'A' Grade men's individual foil, London, 2013, and Leon Paul Cup men's individual foil, 2013. (1) (Photos: Graham Morrison)

109

BECOMING A HIGH PERFORMANCE FENCER

Assorted photographs from the Eden Cup men's individual foil, London, 2013, and Leon Paul Cup men's individual foil, 2013. (2) (Photos: Graham Morrison)

BECOMING A HIGH PERFORMANCE FENCER

with a lesson, the coach should choose actions that are often used by the pupil and should try to boost the pupil's confidence, avoiding direct or excessive correction. (Lukovich, 2013)

You cannot be ready to compete under stress unless you have trained under stress. Smart athletes train their minds to be ready for the unique pressure of the biggest competitions. (Kogler, 2005, p.216) You must be prepared to act at all times. For example, when an offensive action fails to produce an immediate result, there can be a break in the timing. The first person to take advantage of this pause can score a hit.

Strength and Endurance

It is not necessary to develop lots of additional strength, simply to make thrusts that exceed 500 grams-force at foil and 750 grams-force at épée. Whatever strength is needed can be attained through the consistent practising of technique. It is perhaps more important to develop the muscles of the torso. Fencing

The first person to react to a break in play can take the advantage. The Glasgow Open, 2014.

111

BECOMING A HIGH PERFORMANCE FENCER

Sabreurs at close quarters. Stephen Rocks, the man acting as referee in the foreground, went on to win the gold medal in the men's individual sabre at the Glasgow Open, 2014.

FENCING-SPECIFIC ENDURANCE

Resistance to perceptual fatigue:
- Closely watching the opponent.
- Speed and accuracy of perception.
- A high level of attention.
- Fast and appropriate reaction.
- Cognitive or mental fatigue.
- Trying to assess the opponent's tactics.
- Fast analysis of the opponent's and one's own movements.
- Choosing the right tactics.
- Drawing immediate conclusions during and after the bout.

Emotional Fatigue:
- State of anxiety.
- Stressful situations.
- Desire to win.
- Trying to avoid failure.
- Joy, despair and hope.
- Lack of confidence, etc.

And, for a trained fencer, the least important factor is 'physical' fatigue.
(Prof. Zbigniew Czajkowski cited in SSTT, 2011, p.117)

alone will not provide this and the muscles of the back play a huge role in supporting the fencer's posture. (Lukovich, 2013) The need for good core stability is essential when under pressure, particularly when fencers move closer together.

Fencers' short-term endurance can be measured by fencing a bout, mid-term endurance by fencing a round and long-term endurance by fencing a competition. (Lukovich, 2013) It is also important to develop endurance specific to the act of fencing itself, as shown in the panel entitled Fencing-Specific Endurance.

Technique

'Fencing demands intense concentration, not because great strength is needed but because the actions involved are complex. Concentration is also important because it requires and helps to develop associated mental qualities such as judgement in making decisions, determination in achieving a result (whether it be a touch or winning a bout), self-control in not giving into the opponent's attempt to disrupt one's game or concentration and quick thinking in finding the right tactic.' (Alaux, 1975, p.172)

Good fencing technique begins with an efficient and comfortable on guard position, which is influenced by the size and proportions of the whole body. A wide on guard position is stable but less mobile than a narrow guard. We may search for a more stable, secure base when preparing to parry. In front of the rear line of the piste, we tend to use a wider stance in order to be harder to move back. Each individual finds the optimum angle for the torso in relation to the fencing line. The painted lines and the side lines of the piste can make the fencing line visible to students (Lukovich, 2013)

Wojciechowski (n.d., pp.27–29) suggests the heels do not have to be on one line providing the rear foot is on the line of the front foot heel, rear foot toes pointing slightly forward. You do not have to fence exactly on the fencing line but you should feel where it is.

Hand/Arm Coordination and Footwork

Lukovich (2013, p.89) informs us: 'The aim of footwork is *keeping the distance, advancing, gaining ground, changing situation or position, developing actions into hits, creating touches.*'

Footwork is made up of steps, jumps, lunges, flèches and combinations of all these. Half-steps can be used for changing cadence and rhythm, as well as gaining momentum in combinations. Half-steps that stop suddenly may be the products of sudden changes created in bouts. Crossover steps are synonymous with normal walking behaviour and allow for continuous movement and rapidly changing distance. (Lukovich, 2013) The crossover step has the advantage of covering more ground but the fencer is easily 'wrong-footed' if the movement is mistimed. (SSTT, 2011)

With the step forward, the front foot lifts and straightens, toes near to the floor, then rolls forward, landing on the floor, touching first with the heel at the intended step distance. The freed energy from the rear leg pushes the body, which is already in motion, forward and fixes the size of the step. The amount of toe lift depends on the size of the step. The step forward should be finished quickly with the rear foot, which also stays close to the ground. We tend to take shorter steps in a high on guard position and longer steps in a lower on guard position. Distance can be adjusted closely with tiny, stamping steps. (Lukovich, 2013)

The right time to straighten the sword arm, in relation to the foot moving forward, depends on the distance between the fencers and the opponent's reaction time. With a simple first intention attack from inside the opponent's reaction time, the straightening of the sword arm will be prior to the commencement of a foot action. However, if the attacker attempts the same action outside the opponent's reaction time, then the chances of success are poor due to the fact the attacker has signalled his/her intentions and the defender has time to respond. An attack from a distance just outside the opponent's reaction time should be thought of as a long attack with an unknown ending. In such circumstances, the footwork starts first, followed by the gradual straightening of the sword arm. Then, in the closing stages of the lunge when the attacker is within the opponent's reaction time, the sword arm accelerates to overtake the leading foot, the hit landing just before the front foot lands. (SSTT, 2011)

The same technique was taught to Prof. Bert Bracewell by a leading French coach (cited in Rogers, 2013, p.136): 'Start by kicking the front leg forward. The sword arm will be straight by the time the front foot reaches the ground. This has a peculiar timing, since the sword hand overtakes the front foot. The emphasis here is on the terrific speed of the straightening arm and acceleration of the point.' In describing the types of lunge used in sabre, Borysiuk (2009, pp.52–53) refers to this type of action as an 'accelerating lunge' that is used in simple attacks, compound attacks and attacks with an unknown final. His illustration shows the attacker beginning the action with the front foot, the sword arm held back, preparing for an explosive finish.

Footwork is a form of preparation. In the French school of fencing there are three categories of preparation worth mentioning:

- Making and breaking ground (stepping forward and backward).
- Attacks on the blade (attaques-au-fer).
- Takings of the blade (prises-de-fer).

(SSTT, 2011)

Coaching

We can teach fencers how to do things but then we attempt to develop and improve these abilities. This 'improvement' is what coaching is all about. The simplest way to construct a coaching lesson is to break it down into parts (a number of examples follow). The ultimate test of good coaching is that a pupil should be able to use a stroke successfully in a competition environment having first done so in a training environment. In order to make this happen the coach must establish the level of technique required and then put the pupil under pressure. This is achieved by varying distance and timing, correcting errors and building up the pressure to the point where technique breaks down, then immediately reducing the pressure so the pupil becomes successful again. (SSTT, 2011)

Fencing develops many coordination abilities that allow all of this to happen:

- Motor educability (the ability to learn new strokes and change old motor habits).
- Motor control (the ability to direct one's movements precisely).
- Motor adaptability (the ability to adapt fencing actions in unpredictable situations).

(Prof. Zbigniew Czajkowski cited in SSTT, 2011, p.116)

Instinctive motor habits have to be ovecome

when learning new technique. Forcing speed ahead of time can lead to false motor habits. Trying too hard can ruin the order of the muscles involved in an action as well as involve the use of muscles not required at all. So, if the student starts to make mistakes, reduce the speed. It also is important to recognize that things learned in lessons cannot be used in exactly the same way in real fencing situations. Every opponent is different and situations are only similar to one other. (Lukovich, 2013)

In an individual fencing lesson, the fencing master can play the role of the coach (formally), training partner or the opponent. The atmosphere of a lesson is largely influenced by the coach's personality. Hand and arm technique can be perfected from close distance, coordination of hand and feet from middle and long distances. Lunges and flèches may be done on the spot, teaching the fencer how to launch them forcefully, while lessons with mobility teach a fencer to keep distance, the various types of footwork necessary to keeping distance and how to develop and execute actions while in motion. Defence without retreat increases parrying skills. Counter-attacks (by the coach) heighten the reflexes and shorten reaction time. (Lukovich, 2013) To develop technique requires regular practice, attention and concentration, and constant correction. (Alaux, 1975)

Lukovich outlines some of his thoughts in the panel entitled The Individual Lesson.

Tactics

Tactics can be described as the correct application of the actions available to the fencer in order to win or achieve the best possible result. Tactical solutions may be premeditated, following observation of an opponent's

---

THE INDIVIDUAL LESSON

The lesson:

- Gives style, form and character to a fencer's movement.
- Requires the fencer to become accustomed to changing conditions and thus creates a type of adapting mechanism.
- Develops most of the abilities in actual association with one another.
- Gives a boost and reason for the fencer to find his/her unique way of expressing him/herself.

It provides far-reaching opportunity for:

- Customized work.
- Individual treatment.
- Becoming familiar with the student from all aspects.
- Thrashing out the smallest details of technique and tactics.
- Varied use of the methods.

The lesson is determined by the coach's:

- Technical preparedness.
- Feel for tactics.
- Creative imagination.
- Ability to adapt.
- Strength.

(Lukovich, 2013, p.51)

---

habitual actions, or be deduced, after the failure of actions; or be employed as a reaction to an opponent's actions or body language during the preparation of a stroke. (SSTT, 2011)

In the panel entitled Tactical Exercises Done in Pairs, exercises are described that may be practised in a fencing club.

The aim of tactical lessons is to prepare the pupil for combat. In the context of what is

BECOMING A HIGH PERFORMANCE FENCER

> **TACTICAL EXERCISES DONE IN PAIRS**
>
> - Fencing started from an equal score.
> - Fencing with the fencer's lead.
> - Fencing with the opponent leading.
> - Fencing for a single touch to decide the bout.
> - Fencing in the last minute, or seconds, of the bout.
> - Fencing for two out of three victories.
> - Fencing on one or other side of the strip (piste).
> - Fencing on the warning line or on the back line.
> - Fencing without the possibility of retreating.
> - Only counting touches from attacks or parry ripostes.
> - The defender can use only simple or only circular parries.
> - The riposte must always be with opposition or flanconades.
> - The parry is valid only if done in place – or only with breaking the distance.
>
> (Lukovich, 2013, p.170)

being taught, this requires technique that is as close as possible to error-free. Pupils practise the possibilities dictated by given situations. Since tactical situations always offer a variety of possibilities, speed is proportionately decreased by the number of alternatives and the number of alternatives will reflect the pupil's abilities. The strong characteristics of a fencer will influence his/her style, perhaps influencing the percentage of offensive or defensive strokes undertaken. Here, it is the coach's function to create an acceptable balance between the two extremes. (Lukovich, 2013)

Reaction Time

In simple terms, a fencer's reaction time may be regarded as the time it takes to perceive the initiation of a simple attack and to execute a single parry. Reaction times can vary. If an attacker takes the initiative and is very close to the opponent, he/she should be able to hit before the opponent can parry. Here, the attacker is said to be inside the defender's reaction time. Where the distance is such that the defender parries as often as being hit, the attacker is said to be at the defender's reaction time. If this distance is increased beyond the point at which the defender will always parry the attack, the attacker is said to be outside the defender's reaction time. (SSTT, 2011)

A useful exercise is described in the panel entitled Simple and Compound Attacks with One Feint. In this exercise the coach should begin by setting the distance where the pupil is required to step forward in order to get inside the coach's reaction time.

Simple and Compound Attacks with One Feint

A simple reaction is a reaction to a known

BECOMING A HIGH PERFORMANCE FENCER

Simple and Compound Attacks with One Feint

Pupil	Coach
Steps forward. Simple attack (*the attack should hit*). Or	Remains stationary.
Steps forward.	Steps back (small step – only a matter of centimetres); this should position the pupil *outside the coach's reaction time for a simple attack*. i.e. if the pupil attempts to execute a simple attack, the attack should be parried *but inside the coach's reaction time for a compound attack*.
Compound attack (the attack should hit). Or	
Steps forward.	Steps back (normal step) – positioning the pupil *outside the coach's reaction time*. i.e. If the pupil attempts to attack either simple or compound, the attack should be parried.
Desired response is no attack.	
(SSTT, 2011, p.140)	

stimulus with a known motor response. In lessons of this kind, the pupil knows what the stimulus is but not when it will happen. The pupil reacts to a previously agreed move from the coach with a previously agreed response.

A compound reaction may be composed of one or more of the following:

- A choice reaction is a motor response that varies according to the stimulus given. The fencer knows all the answers but does not know which question will be asked.
- A differential reaction is a motor response to only one selected stimulus after discriminating it among other similar stimuli: for example, parrying a 'real' but not a 'false' attack.
- An anticipatory reaction is a motor response made after anticipating the speed and path of a moving object, for example, in coaching the ability to parry a riposte or a counter-riposte.
- An intuitive reaction is a motor response based on intuition, not conscious thought.

(SSTT, 2011)

Simple reaction exercises at foil, sabre and épée:

(a) As the coach steps forward, the pupil executes a direct attack with a lunge.
(b) From a position of engagement, on the coach's movement of the blade, the pupil executes a simple attack with a lunge.
(c) From an extended arm position with the point in-line, as the coach attempts prise-de-fer the pupil executes a dérobement.
(d) On the coach's direct attack, the pupil reacts with a parry-riposte.

(SSTT, 2011)

BECOMING A HIGH PERFORMANCE FENCER

Choice reaction exercises at foil, sabre and épée:

(a) The pupil begins on guard at step-lunge distance and then steps forward with the intention of being just outside the coach's reaction time. The coach launches a simple attack into the pupil's preparation without announcing in advance which line the attack will be directed to. The coach directs the pupil to defend, counter-attack or choose between the two. The pupil takes the most appropriate parry-riposte or counter-attack and then hits. Occasionally, the coach makes a reasonable attempt to parry the pupil's final offensive action but not fast enough to discourage the pupil.

(b) The pupil begins on guard at step-lunge distance and then steps forward with the intention of being just outside the coach's reaction time; launching an 'open-eyes' simple attack with no immediate intention of hitting. If the coach does not respond, the pupil accelerates the lunge and hits (simple attack). If the coach attempts to defend with a parry, the pupil completes the attack by deceiving the parry and hitting into the opening line as shown in the diagrams (compound attack). If the coach attempts to counter-attack, the pupil finishes by parrying the counter-attack and ripostes (counter-time). As a general rule, it is helpful to begin with two choices and work until they are being performed correctly. Substitute one of the choices with a third (new choice) and then work to achieve success with these two. Work by substitution of choice until the pupil is capable of completing three or more variations.

Choice reaction exercise at sabre:

(c) The pupil begins on guard at step-lunge distance and steps forward with a feint to head. If the coach does not respond, the pupil accelerates the attack direct to head with a lunge (simple attack). If the coach attempts to parry quinte, the pupil deceives the parry, hitting into an opening line (compound attack). If the coach attempts to counter-attack, the pupil finishes by parrying the counter-attack and ripostes (counter-time).

(SSTT, 2011, pp.275–278)

If the coach does not respond, the pupil accelerates the lunge.

BECOMING A HIGH PERFORMANCE FENCER

If the coach attempts to defend with a parry, the pupil completes the attack by deceiving the parry and hitting into the opening line.

If the coach attempts to counter-attack, the pupil finishes by parrying the counter-attack and ripostes.

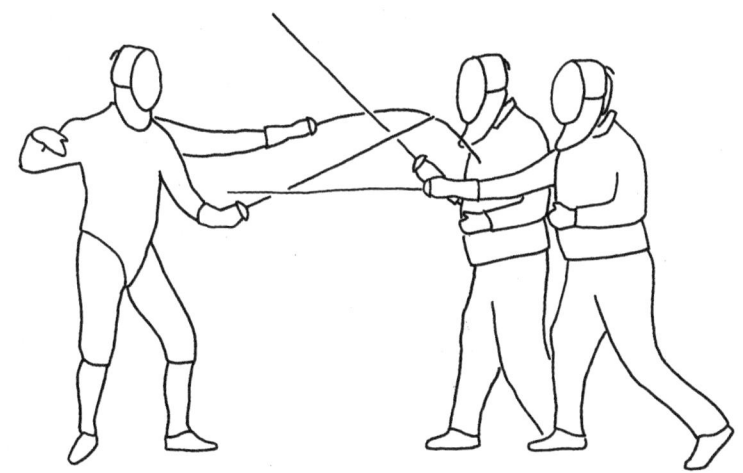

Differential reaction exercises at foil, sabre and épée:

(a) The pupil begins on guard at step-lunge distance and then steps forward with the intention of being just outside the coach's reaction time. The coach launches a *real* simple attack into the pupil's preparation, intending to hit. The pupil must parry-riposte or counter-attack. Alternatively, the coach may launch a *false* simple attack into the pupil's preparation with the intention of reconnaissance/exploration. The pupil must either perform a previously agreed offensive action or ignore the attack and return to the start position.

(b) The pupil begins on guard at step-lunge distance and then steps forward with the intention of being just outside the coach's reaction time. The coach launches a *real* simple attack into the pupil's preparation, intending to hit. The pupil parries the attack, holding the parry and not riposting immediately. The coach responds to being parried by closing the line, anticipating a

direct riposte. The pupil then ripostes into the appropriate opening line. Alternatively, the coach may launch a *false* simple attack into the pupil's preparation with the intention of reconnaissance/exploration. The pupil must either perform a previously agreed offensive action or ignore the attack and return to the start position.
(c) The pupil begins on guard at step-lunge distance and then steps forward with the intention of being just outside the coach's reaction time. The coach launches a *well-executed* simple attack into the pupil's preparation. The pupil does parry-riposte. Alternatively, the coach launches a *poorly executed* simple attack into the pupil's preparation. This can involve exposing the wrist/forearm at sabre/épée or bending the arm during the execution of the attack. The pupil counter-attacks.

(SSTT, 2011, pp.279–281)

Anticipatory reaction exercises at foil, sabre and épée:

(a) The coach attacks from varying start distances and varying speeds of execution. The pupil attempts to parry at just the right moment – not too late to avoid being hit and not too early to avoid the attacker having the opportunity to change direction – hitting into an opening line.
(b) The coach executes first counter-ripostes, varying the speed of execution of both the attack and first counter-riposte, changing the cadence of the first counter-riposte relative to that of the pupil's riposte.

(SSTT, 2011, p.250)

Intuitive reaction exercises at foil, sabre and épée:

(a) The pupil begins in a covered line at lunging distance and beats the blade with the intention of attacking direct. If the coach does nothing, the pupil completes the direct attack. Infrequently and without warning, the coach responds with a previously agreed lateral parry and the pupil must disengage or cut-over.
(b) The pupil begins in a covered line at lunging distance and feints with disengage or cutover, with the intention of hitting. The coach responds to the feint with a parry of quarte, as previously agreed. The pupil completes the compound attack. Alternatively, the coach responds to the feint with a counter-attack, as previously agreed. The pupil does parry-riposte (counter-time).

(SSTT, 2011, pp.283–284)

Adjusting to Your Opponent's Speed

Many coaches and fencers strive to execute actions as quickly as possible. However, slowing down an action can increase the chance of success due to the element of surprise. (SSTT, 2011)

Foil, sabre and épée

(a) The pupil's next task is to use a prise-de-fer to provoke a reaction and then take advantage of it. The coach begins on guard at step-lunge distance; arm straight, point in-line, threatening the target. The pupil steps forward, with a prise-de-fer, slowly, not intending to hit. The coach slips off or evades the prise-de-fer. The pupil beats the blade and lunges fast. Occasionally, the coach makes a reasonable attempt to parry the pupil's final offensive action but not fast enough to discourage the pupil.
(b) Next, the pupil provokes an 'open eyes' attack into a specific final line and then

BECOMING A HIGH PERFORMANCE FENCER

takes advantage of it. The coach is on guard at step-lunge distance in a covered line. The pupil steps forward, opening a line. The coach attempts to hit with an 'open eyes' compound attack. The pupil slowly makes a false parry, drawing the coach into a specific line. The coach finishes quickly into the opening line but the pupil takes a very fast second parry-riposte.

Foil and épée

(c) The aim of this exercise is to change the pace of ripostes and counter-ripostes relative to those of the opponent (coach). The pupil begins on guard in octave at riposting distance and the coach begins on guard in sixte. The coach-pupil responses are as follows: the coach attacks (outside low line) – the pupil parries octave-riposte (by disengage), parries quarte-riposte (direct) – parries quarte-riposte direct, parries quarte-riposte (outside low line) – parries octave-riposte (in opposition through octave). The pupil has to change rhythm relative to that of the coach. The pace/rhythm of the coach's movements may be constant or vary considerably.

(d) The pupil begins on guard with the point threatening the target at riposting distance. As the coach attempts to engage in octave, the pupil does dérobement disengage hit; as shown in the diagram; then sixte and the pupil does dérobement disengage hit; then circular sixte and the pupil does dérobement by counter-disengage hit. The above sequence of attempted engagements may be repeated with the coach adding a bind from quarte to octave at the end, which the pupil deceives by dérobement disengage.

Sabre

(e) The pupil begins on guard with the point threatening the target at riposting distance. As the coach attempts to engage in seconde, the pupil does dérobement disengage hit; then tierce and the pupil

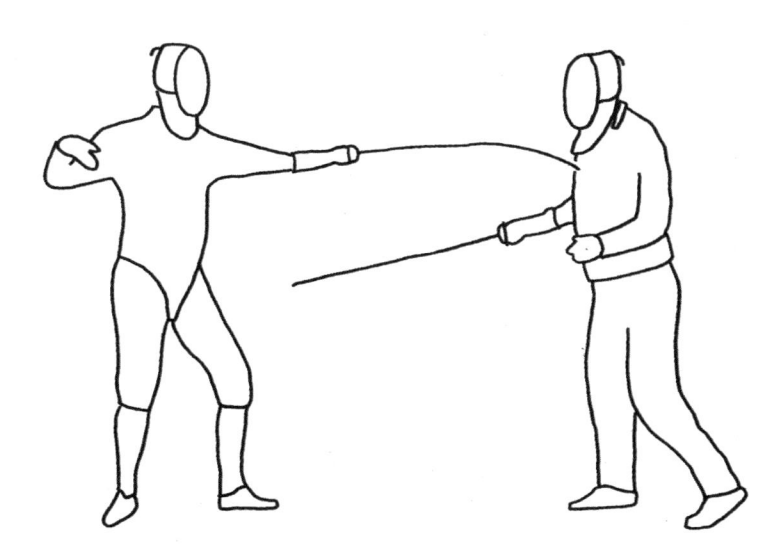

As the coach attempts to engage in octave, the pupil does dérobement disengage hit.

BECOMING A HIGH PERFORMANCE FENCER

Bert Bracewell at Wallace Fencing Academy.

does dérobement disengage hit; then circular tierce and the pupil does dérobement by counter-disengage hit.

(SSTT, 2011, pp.285–287)

(f) A similar exercise at sabre is recounted by Prof. Bert Bracewell, as taught to him by his own coach Prof. Alf Simmonds (cited in Rogers, 2013, p.68): 'The fencer begins in the on guard position at step and lunge distance to target; the hand and blade are forward, point towards the target. The attacker (coach) goes for the blade twice, moving forward. The fencer deceives the blade both times, placing the point lightly on the target… This time, the fencer begins in seconde… The attacker goes for the blade, twice moving forward. The fencer deceives the blade both times, placing the point lightly on the target… The fencer begins in seconde and must evade all the opponent's (coach's) blade movements by moving the sword hand from seconde to tierce, quinte, prime, quarte, and finishing with a tierce riposte with the point, ensuring that all the guards are formed correctly… Next the opponent (coach) holds the sabre in the left hand and repeats (the previous exercise)…'

Area Being Threatened

When experiencing many bouts in succession at a fencing competition, it is helpful if you can determine which area of the target is likely to be under threat at any one time.

During an opponent's preparation or offensive action, there is often sufficient time to discern which line is most likely to be under threat. This 'feeling' may be based upon experience or observation of clues provided by the opponent. Fencers who are proficient at this skill are more likely to be confident in defence and may, as a result, spend more of their time preparing offensive action. (SSTT, 2011)

Foil

(a) The pupil begins on guard at step-lunge distance and then steps forward with the intention of being just outside the coach's reaction time. The coach attacks by disengage with angulation into the sixte line and the pupil parries sixte-riposte. Next, the coach attacks direct to the outside low line and the pupil parries circular sixte, or octave, and ripostes. Next, the coach attacks direct to the high line and the pupil parries quarte, circular sixte, or octave, and ripostes. Begin with two choices and work until they are being performed correctly. Substitute one of the choices with a third (new choice) and then work to achieve success with these two. Work by substitution of choice until the pupil is capable of completing three or more variations.

(b) The pupil begins on guard in sixte at step-lunge distance and steps forward, attacking directly with a lunge. The coach begins on guard in octave and parries sixte, riposting with angulation in the sixte line; the pupil parries sixte and ripostes into the low line. Next, the coach parries sixte and ripostes in the outside low line; or, parries quarte and ripostes in the outside low line. The pupil parries octave and ripostes in the high line. Next, the coach parries quarte and ripostes direct in the high line. The pupil parries quarte and ripostes direct in the high line. Occasionally, the coach makes a reasonable attempt to parry the pupil's final offensive action but not fast enough to discourage the pupil.

Épée

(c) The pupil begins on guard at step-lunge distance and then steps forward with the intention of being just outside the coach's reaction time. The coach attacks to leg and the pupil counter-attacks to wrist/arm. Next, the coach attacks by disengage in opposition to upper arm/shoulder and the pupil parries sixte-riposte in opposition to body, or counter-attacks in opposition in sixte to body. Next, the coach attacks direct to body and the pupil parries quarte, circular sixte, or octave and ripostes; or counter-attacks to arm. The coach may specify any of the options that are available or leave the choice up to the pupil.

(d) The pupil begins on guard in sixte at step-lunge distance and steps forward with a direct attack to forearm. The coach begins in octave, parries sixte-riposte in opposition to upper arm and the pupil parries sixte-riposte in opposition to shoulder. Next, the coach parries quarte-riposte by bind to body and the pupil cedes to quarte and ripostes to body or opposes to octave and ripostes to body. Next, the coach parries circular octave with riposte in opposition to leg and the pupil parries octave in opposition with riposte to body or foot.

Sabre

(e) The pupil begins on guard in tierce at step-lunge distance and then steps forward with the intention of being just outside the coach's reaction time. The coach attacks direct to flank and the pupil parries

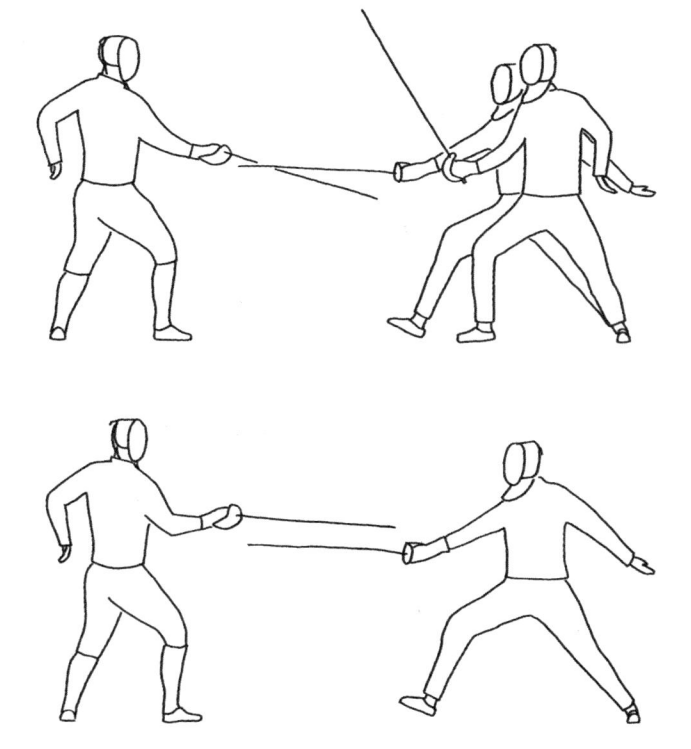

The coach attacks direct to flank and the pupil parries seconde-riposte or counter-attacks to wrist.

seconde-riposte or counter-attacks to wrist. Next, the coach attacks direct to head and the pupil parries quinte-riposte or counter-attacks to wrist. Next, the coach attacks direct to chest and the pupil parries quarte-riposte or counter-attacks to wrist. The possible actions of the coach and pupil are not limited to those stated.
(SSTT, 2011, pp.288–293)

Potentially, all offensive actions may be delivered with angulation. Angulation should be left to the last possible moment. By hitting at an angle near to 90 degrees (foil and épée) the point is less likely to slip off. There will be a certain surprise value if the opponent truly feels that the line is covered. (SSTT, 2011)

'Open Eyes'

It has been said that: 'The character of an "open eyes" attack is that of a progressive reconnaissance action, not knowing when or where it will end. The fencer therefore reacts instantly to the changing conditions of the opponent.' (SSTT, 2011, p.265)

Foil and Épée

(a) The pupil begins on guard in sixte at step-lunge distance. The coach's sword arm is straight, with the point in-line. The pupil steps forward and engages the coach's blade in a quarte-octave bind with a lunge. The coach cedes to quarte, the pupil slips off the parry and completes the attack by disengage. Next, the coach does not react and the pupil completes the attack in opposition. Next, the coach evades the attempted bind with a dérobement and the pupil responds with parry-riposte before completing the lunge.

(b) The pupil begins on guard in sixte at step-lunge distance; the coach's sword arm is straight, with the point in-line. The pupil steps forward with a feint into the low line then engages the coach's blade in a quarte-octave bind with a lunge. The coach does not react and the pupil completes the attack into the high line. Next, the coach

The fencer reacts instantly to the changing conditions of the opponent, as simulated by the coach's hand movements.

parries octave and the pupil completes the attack by disengage into the high line. Next, the coach counter-attacks direct in the high line, forcing the pupil to move from the feint to parry-riposte (counter-time). Next, as the coach steps back, the pupil completes the attack into the high-line with a flèche.

Sabre

(c) The pupil begins on guard in the offensive/defensive position at step-lunge distance and steps forward with a feint to chest. The coach, who is also on guard in the offensive/defensive position, does not react and the pupil completes the direct attack to head with a lunge. Next, the coach parries quarte, responding to the feint and the coach completes the compound attack feint chest-flank with a lunge. Next, the coach counter-attacks to wrist and the pupil moves from the feint to parry-riposte (counter-time). Next, as the coach steps back, the pupil steps forward and does any of the previous three options.

(SSTT, 2011, pp.317–319)

Assessment of Distance

Distance is an important element of all offensive and defensive actions. It is also important to recognize and respond to an opponent who is attempting to control distance. The failure to assess distance correctly can be seen in people who over-lunge, lunge short, overextend the sword arm when hitting or finish too close to the opponent after a

The failure to assess distance correctly can be seen in people who over-lunge. (Photo: Graham Morrison)

preparation or change of direction. (SSTT, 2011)

Judging the distance separating opponents is one of the primary senses required for combat. Fencers tend to calibrate this distance based on the height of the body and the length of the limbs. The distance to be crossed depends, more or less, on physical speed. Distance modifies hand-foot coordination, in conjunction with various blade movements. (Lukovich, 2013)

Paul, et al. (2012, p.103) advises that: 'At the advanced level, you should be able to "feel", or intuitively sense, distance. Distance is also understood as a type of "pressure" from the opponent… Closing distance puts pressure on to your opponent; opening the distance creates a vacuum…'

Foil, sabre and épée

(a) The pupil begins on guard in sixte (sabre – tierce) at step-lunge distance. The coach is on guard in octave (sabre-seconde) and responds randomly as the pupil steps forward with the intention of getting just inside the coach's reaction time. As the pupil steps forward, the coach steps forward, attempting to engage the blade in sixte (sabre – tierce) and the pupil attacks by disengage, with no further footwork required. Next, as the pupil steps forward, the coach remains stationary, attempting to engage the blade in sixte (sabre – tierce) and the pupil attacks by disengage with a lunge. Next, as the pupil steps forward, the coach takes a half-step back, attempting to engage the blade in sixte (sabre – tierce) and the pupil attacks compound with a lunge, as the coach responds to the feint. Next, as the pupil steps forward, the coach takes a normal step back and does nothing. The pupil steps forward again and at this point any of the previous three options may be introduced. The coach should specify which option or combination of options.

(b) The pupil begins on guard in sixte (sabre – tierce) at step-lunge distance and steps forward with a direct attack, lunging deliberately short. The coach remains stationary and does quarte-riposte direct and the pupil remains on the lunge and does quarte counter-riposte direct. Next, the coach steps back with quarte-riposte direct and the pupil recovers forward and parries quarte. Immediately on being parried, the coach steps back and closes a previously agreed line. The pupil does indirect first counter-riposte with a lunge.

(c) The pupil begins on guard in sixte (sabre – tierce) at step-lunge distance and steps forward with the intention of being just outside the coach's reaction time. The coach attacks direct into the pupil's preparation, then does nothing and the pupil parries quarte-riposte direct. Next, immediately after the pupil parries quarte, the coach recovers back on guard and closes a previously agreed line. The pupil completes the indirect riposte with a lunge. Occasionally, the coach makes a reasonable attempt to parry the pupil's final offensive action but not fast enough to discourage the pupil.

(SSTT, 2011, pp.297–298)

Touch and Visual Observation

Sentiment du fer is the tactile perception, even through brief contact with the opponent's blade, of how they are reacting. This skill distinguishes between an opponent who parries and does not riposte, parries and delays the riposte or parries and ripostes immediately (see diagram). As parries are

BECOMING A HIGH PERFORMANCE FENCER

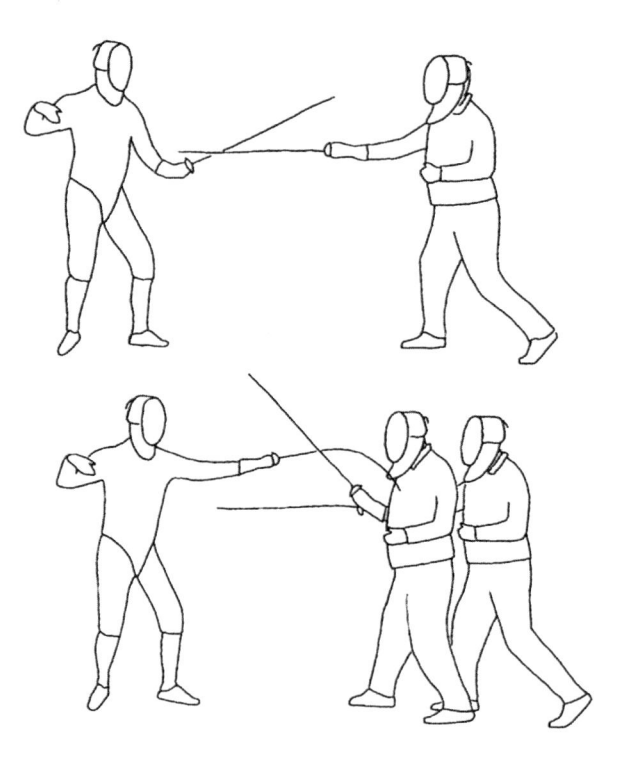

Sentiment de fer distinguishes between an opponent who parries and does not riposte, parries and delays the riposte, or parries and ripostes immediately.

formed, each should feel subtly different. Other examples of where the 'feeling' of the blade is important are engagements, change of engagements and prises-de-fer. Visual observation is also important. The ability to foresee an opponent's moves makes it easier to choose a suitable counter-move and there is likely to be a faster speed of reaction compared with that against a move that is visually unforeseen.

(SSTT, 2011)

Foil

(a) The pupil's aim is to assess visually how the coach responds and react accordingly. The pupil begins on guard in sixte at step-lunge distance and the coach is on guard in sixte. The pupil steps forward with the intention of being just inside the coach's reaction time. The coach does not react and the pupil completes the direct attack with a lunge. Next, as the pupil steps forward, the coach attempts to engage the blade in sixte or quarte and the pupil completes the attack by disengage with a lunge. Next, as the pupil steps forward, the coach takes a half-step back and attempts to engage the blade in sixte; the pupil feints direct and disengages with a lunge. Next, as the pupil steps forward, the coach takes a half-step back and attempts to engage the blade with a circular sixte action; the pupil feints direct and counter-disengages with a lunge. Next, as the pupil steps forward, the coach attacks direct and the pupil parries quarte-riposte direct.

(b) The pupil's aim is to assess through touch how the coach responds and react accordingly. The pupil begins on guard in sixte at step-lunge distance and the coach is on guard in quarte. The pupil steps forward, the coach does not react. The pupil does a one-two attack, disengage-disengage with a step forward and the coach parries sixte, circular sixte with the pupil hitting the coach before he/she completes the circular parry; or the coach parries sixte-quarte and ripostes direct with the pupil parrying quarte-riposte (first counter-riposte) direct. Next, as the pupil steps forward, the coach attacks direct with a lunge. The pupil does a quarte-riposte direct as the coach parries circular sixte, with the pupil hitting the coach before he/she completes the circular parry; or the coach parries quarte-riposte direct (first counter-riposte), with the pupil parrying quarte-riposte direct (second counter-riposte). The coach should either specify options or trust the pupil to react accordingly.

Sabre

(c) The pupil's aim is to assess visually how the coach responds and react accordingly. The pupil begins on guard in the offensive/defensive position at step-lunge distance and steps forward, intending to be just inside the coach's reaction time. The coach, who is on guard in the offensive/defensive position, does not react and the pupil completes the direct attack to head with a lunge. Next, as the pupil steps forward, the coach closes the quarte line and the pupil completes the direct attack to head (or flank) with a lunge. For the next part, the coach reacts to the pupil's feints by taking a previously agreed parry. As the pupil steps forward, the coach takes a half-step back and the pupil completes the compound attack feint to head, cut to chest with a lunge. Next, as the pupil steps forward, the coach takes a half-step back, closing the quarte line, and the pupil completes the compound attack feint to flank, cut head with a lunge. Next, as the pupil steps forward, the coach attacks direct to chest and the pupil parries quarte-riposte direct.

(d) The pupil's aim is to assess through touch how the coach responds and react accordingly. The pupil begins on guard in the offensive/defensive position at step-lunge distance and steps forward. The coach does not react and the pupil attacks compound feint chest-flank. The coach reacts to the feint (with quarte) and the pupil completes the compound attack. Alternatively, the coach parries quarte-tierce and ripostes to flank; the pupil parries tierce and counter-ripostes to head. Next, as the pupil steps forward, the coach attacks direct to chest and the pupil parries quarte-riposte to head. The coach attempts to parry the riposte but it gets through.

Épée

(e) The pupil's aim is to assess visually how the coach responds and react accordingly. The pupil begins on guard in sixte at step-lunge distance and the coach is on guard in octave. The pupil steps forward with the intention of being just inside the coach's reaction time. The coach does not react and the pupil attacks direct to arm with a lunge. Next, as the pupil steps forward, the coach attempts to engage the blade and the pupil attacks by disengage with a lunge. Next, as the pupil steps forward, the coach takes a half-step back and the pupil attacks to wrist with a lunge. The coach reacts to the pupil's attack by taking a previously agreed semi-circular or circular parry and the pupil redoubles with disengage to arm. Next, as the pupil steps forward, the coach attacks

direct to arm and the pupils parries circular sixte-riposte direct, or counter-attacks.
(f) The pupil's aim is to assess through touch how the coach responds and react accordingly. The pupil begins on guard in sixte at step-lunge distance and the coach is on guard in octave. The pupil steps forward, the coach does not react and the pupil attacks to wrist. The choices of responses are as follows:

- The coach parries sixte, leaving the line slightly exposed and the pupil redoubles with angulation.
- The coach parries sixte-riposte by disengage and the pupil remises.
- The coach parries sixte (fully) and the pupil redoubles by disengage to arm or upper leg.
- The coach steps back parrying sixte and the pupil recovers forward with disengage to arm (forward reprise).

(SSTT, 2011, pp.299–304)

Hitting Into an Opening Line

If a fencer is attacking into an opening line of quarte, then the defending fencer must be closing another line; either sixte or octave (sabre – tierce or seconde). Before the defender can parry, he/she must recognize which line is being threatened, stop opening in that line and begin to form a parry to protect the line under threat, thus increasing the time available for the attacker to become successful. Hence, attacking into a line that is being uncovered is more effective than attacking into an (already) open line where the opponent's blade is stationary. Recognition of an opening line is based primarily on visual analysis.

(SSTT, 2011)

Foil

(a) The pupil begins on guard in sixte at step-lunge distance and the coach is on guard in octave. The pupil steps forward with a feint direct, the coach closes the line of quarte and the pupil disengages with a lunge (compound attack). Next, the pupil steps forward with a feint direct, the coach closes the line of sixte and the pupil disengages with a lunge (compound attack). Next, as the pupil steps forward with a feint direct, the coach takes a half-step back parrying quarte, or sixte. The pupil steps forward with a feint disengage and lunges with a further disengage (compound attack) as the coach reacts to the pupil's second disengage by taking a previously agreed simple parry.

(b) The pupil begins on guard in sixte at step-lunge distance and the coach is on guard in octave. The pupil steps forward, the coach attacks direct into this preparation and the pupil parries quarte. The choices of responses are as follows:

- The coach reacts immediately to being parried by closing the quarte line and the pupil ripostes by disengage.
- The coach reacts immediately to being parried by changing the engagement to sixte and the pupil ripostes by counter-disengage.
- The coach parries quarte-riposte direct (first counter-riposte) and the pupil parries quarte-riposte direct (second counter-riposte).
- The coach parries quarte-riposte in the outside low line (first counter-riposte) and the pupil parries octave-riposte by disengage in the high line (second counter-riposte).

Begin with two choices and work until they

are being performed correctly. Substitute one of the choices with a third (new choice) and then work to achieve success with these two. Work by substitution of choice until the pupil is capable of completing three or more variations.

Sabre

(c) The coach and pupil begin on guard in an offensive/defensive position at step-lunge distance. As the pupil steps forward, the coach attacks direct to head and the pupil parries quinte. The coach reacts with a parry, anticipating a direct riposte and the pupil ripostes into an opening line.

(d) The coach and pupil begin on guard in an offensive/defensive position at step-lunge distance. The pupil steps forward with a feint to head, the coach stop-cuts under the wrist and recovers to a covered line. The pupil parries seconde and ripostes into an opening line.

Épée

(e) The coach and pupil begin on guard in sixte at step-lunge distance. The pupil steps forward with a beat, feint attack under the wrist. The coach withdraws the sword hand and the pupil attacks direct to body with a lunge. Next, the coach parries circular sixte and the pupil renews by disengage to arm, body, leg or foot, with a lunge or completes a compound attack to upper arm with a counter-disengage lunge. Next, the coach parries octave and the pupil renews by disengage with a lunge or completes a compound attack to upper arm with a disengage lunge.

(f) The coach and pupil begin on guard in sixte at step-lunge distance. The coach moves between sixte and quarte, changing engagement constantly, then pauses.

Then, the coach steps forward with a feint of a coulé in sixte or quarte to arm and the pupil attacks by disengage with lunge in opposition to arm or body. Next, the coach steps forward with an engagement and the pupil attacks by disengage with lunge to arm or body. Next, the coach steps forward with a change of engagement and the pupil attacks by counter-disengage with lunge to arm or body.

(SSTT, 2011, pp.305–310)

Timing of an Action

Speed and technical proficiency is fine but an element of surprise is even better. Choosing an appropriate surprise action and its timing requires careful reading of the opponent. (SSTT, 2011)

Foil and Épée

(a) The pupil begins on guard in sixte at step-lunge distance and the coach is on guard in octave. The coach steps forward in quarte, the pupil does not react and they start again. Next, the coach steps forward, indicating an attempt to engage in quarte, then opens the line by moving to sixte (see diagrams). The pupil does not react to the attempted engagement but attacks direct into the second opening line. Next, the coach steps forward, indicating an attempt to engage in quarte, then changes the engagement to sixte. The pupil does not react to the attempted engagement but attacks by counter-disengage into the second opening line. Next, the coach steps forward in sixte and the pupil attacks by disengage. In each of these exercises the coach should, in the early stages, move his/her sword in a consistent manner. As the pupil improves, the coach

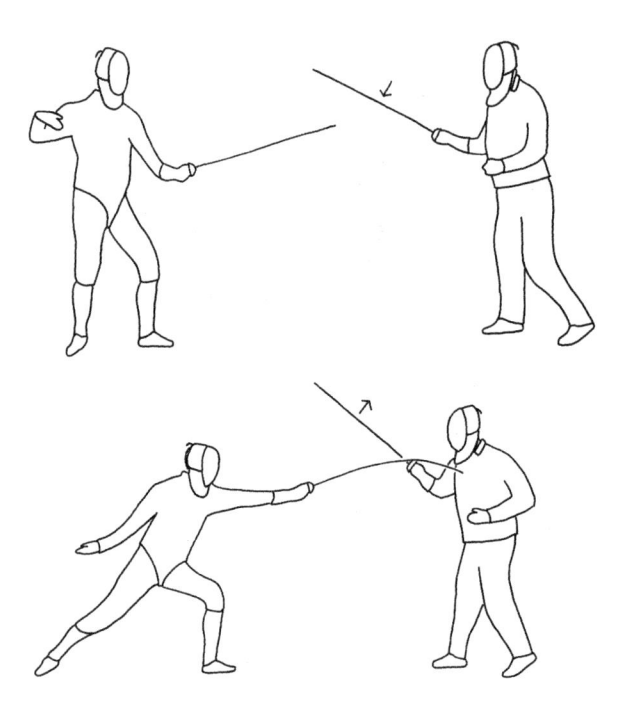

The coach steps forward, indicating an attempt to engage in quarte, then opens the line by moving to sixte.

should vary the speed and rhythm of his/her actions.

Sabre

(b) The coach and pupil begin on guard in an offensive/defensive position at step-lunge distance. The coach moves randomly between tierce and quarte. The pupil does not react and then they start again. Next, the coach moves the blade as before then, at any moment he/she steps forward into seconde, tierce, quarte or quinte and the pupil attacks direct to any available target. Occasionally, the coach makes a reasonable attempt to parry the pupil's final offensive action but not fast enough to frustrate the pupil.

(c) The coach and pupil begin on guard in an offensive/defensive position at step-lunge distance. As the pupil steps forward, the coach indicates a cut to head, almost straightening the sword arm, then recovers to tierce or quarte and the pupil attacks direct to any available target. Next, as the pupil steps forward, the coach closes the line to tierce or quarte and the pupil attacks direct to any available target. In each of these exercises, the coach should, in the early stages, move his/her sword in a consistent manner. As the pupil improves, the coach should vary the speed and rhythm of his/her actions.

(d) The coach and pupil begin on guard in an offensive/defensive position at step-lunge distance. As the pupil steps forward, the coach moves the sabre between different guards and the pupil does not react. They start again. As the pupil steps forward, the coach moves between different guards and the pupil launches a direct attack into the transition.

(e) The coach and pupil begin on guard in an offensive/defensive position at step-lunge distance. The coach steps forward, indicating a feint in any line, then recovers to the offensive/defensive position and the pupil does not react. They start again. The coach steps forward, indicating a feint to head, almost straightening the arm, and then they respond as follows:

- The coach recovers to tierce as the pupil attacks direct with a lunge into the available target.
- The coach moves to tierce and then attempts to parry quarte as the pupil attacks compound with a lunge.
- The coach steps back with the point in-line as the pupil attacks beat to wrist with a lunge.
- The coach steps back and then moves to quarte as the pupil attacks compound with a step-lunge.

(SSTT, 2011, pp.311–316)

Role-Play

In a role-play type of lesson the coach plays the part of a particular type of opponent. The coach begins by deciding who should initiate the sequence: coach or pupil. For example, the pupil can execute preparatory movements, such as feints or different types of footwork, looking for the coach to respond with an appropriate counter-action. Alternatively, the coach can execute preparatory movements, looking for the pupil to respond. In either case, the pupil is encouraged to take the upper hand and outwit the coach, scoring a hit. (SSTT, 2011)

Foil, Sabre and Épée

(a) In what follows, the coach plays the part of an inexperienced opponent, who may respond erratically. The pupil begins on guard in octave (sabre – seconde) at step-lunge distance and the coach is in a covered position. The pupil steps forward into sixte (sabre – tierce), indicating an attempt to take the blade, and the coach makes a false attack with a lunge. The pupil steps back from the attack. After a short pause, both resume their starting positions. Next, the pupil steps forward with a deliberate attempt to take the

In a role-play type of lesson, the coach plays the part of a particular type of opponent. The coach moves in too close without warning and the pupil must adjust and respond.

blade and the coach attacks with a lunge with the intention of hitting. The pupil then responds with parry-riposte or counter-attack and hits.
(b) The pupil begins on guard in octave (sabre – seconde) at step-lunge distance and the coach is in a covered position. The coach steps forward and attacks with a short lunge and the pupil steps back with a half-parry. After a short pause, both resume their starting positions. Next, the coach steps forward and attacks compound with the intention of hitting. The pupil steps back taking successive parries-riposte or counter-attacks and hits.
(c) In what follows, the coach responds in different ways to the pupil's preparation. The pupil begins on guard in octave (sabre – seconde) at step-lunge distance and the coach is in a covered position. The pupil does a preparatory attack step forward half-lunge deliberately short in order to observe the coach's probable response. The coach steps back with a half-parry. After a short pause, both resume their starting positions. Next, the pupil attacks compound with step forward and lunge, with considerable increase in tempo. The coach attempts to step back with the same half-parry as the pupil finishes the compound attack.
(d) The pupil begins on guard in octave (sabre – seconde) at step-lunge distance and the coach is in a covered position. The pupil does a preparatory attack step forward half-lunge deliberately short in order to observe the coach's probable response. The coach steps back with a half-parry, this time indicating a riposte. After a short pause, both resume their starting positions. Next, the pupil attacks compound with step forward and lunge, with considerable increase in tempo. The coach attempts to step back, taking successive parries and ripostes with the intention of hitting. The pupil completes the compound attack, followed by the first counter-riposte.
(e) The pupil begins on guard in octave (sabre – seconde) at step-lunge distance and the coach is in a covered position. The pupil does a preparatory attack step forward half-lunge deliberately short in order to observe the coach's probable response. The coach steps back, indicating a counter-attack. After a short pause, both resume their starting positions. Next, the pupil attacks compound with step forward and lunge, with considerable increase in tempo. The coach attempts to step back with the same counter-attack with the intention of hitting. The pupil does parry-riposte (counter-time), executed during the timing of the attack. Occasionally, the coach makes a reasonable attempt to parry the pupil's final offensive action but not fast enough to discourage the pupil.

(SSTT, 2011, pp.294–295)

Periodization/Training Cycles

At any fencing competition you can be surrounded by people and then be required to persevere on your own. It is hard to characterize how one feels under these circumstances unless you experience these things for yourself. One thing is very clear, however: in order to cope and compete at your best, it is necessary to get organized and plan ahead.

No athlete can train at maximum intensity all the time and must make room for rest and recovery. This leads us to a system sometimes referred to as periodization or training cycles. (Borysiuk, 2009) Periodization is simply a term applied to planning training sessions and arranging them in an organized fashion. This tends to involve planning

BECOMING A HIGH PERFORMANCE FENCER

Sometimes you must persevere on your own. The Glasgow Open, 2014.

training programmes in successive small units. In each planned segment, various aspects of skills training, speed, strength, stamina and so on may be considered. There is often a preparation period and a competition period. (Track and Field Coach, n.d.) In this preparation period, fencers must build both an aerobic and anaerobic base, as well as developing general and fencing-specific coordination and decision-making. In this they must move from perfecting separate fencing techniques to combining these techniques, using them in tactical situations and even preparing to fence specific opponents. (Borysiuk, 2009)

You will need to begin with an annual plan for your competitions and get advice on a physical training plan to match. In order to build up your national ranking points you are likely to enter a number of open competitions throughout the year: some will be FIE (Fédération Internationale d'Escrime) international events. Humans are territorial creatures who usually feel at their best on home ground, conditions that are rarely met at international events. (Paul, et al., 2012)

Taking Part in FIE Competitions

The latest (up-to-date) version of the rules applicable to FIE competitions is available from its website fie.ch/Fencing/Rules.aspx.

THE INTERNATIONAL COMPETITION CIRCUIT (ABRIDGED)

- Different amounts of world ranking points are available for each of the different types of competitions… You will need an FIE licence to compete and generally you apply for this via your national federation…
- You must be entered by your national federation… and each of these competitions have different rules on how many fencers from each country are permitted to take part. There are sometimes additional requirements for the national body to provide referees based on the number of fencers they send.
- …at the Senior (Open) World Championships, entries are limited to four fencers per weapon per nation for the individual events and one team per weapon per nation for the team events. At the Junior World Championships, only three fencers can fence per nation in the individual event.
- In individual Category A competitions, both Senior and Junior, for each weapon each national federation may enter a maximum of twelve fencers. For competitions in Europe, the organizing country may enter up to twenty fencers, plus more if they are needed to make up the poule numbers. Outside Europe, this rises to thirty fencers plus the number needed to make up the poules.
- For Grand Prix competitions, entries are limited to a maximum of eight fencers per weapon per country. The organizing country may enter up to twelve fencers, plus the number of fencers needed to make up the poule, up to a maximum of twenty fencers.
- Satellite competitions are not limited by entry but usually there is a requirement to provide one or more referees if more than four fencers are entered.

(Usher, in Paul, et al., 2012, p.90)

BECOMING A HIGH PERFORMANCE FENCER

At the time of writing, the following age restrictions were held to apply:

- No fencer is allowed to take part in an official event of the FIE unless he or she is at least thirteen years old on 1 January in the year of the competition.
- Fencers taking part in the official FIE Cadet competitions must be under seventeen years old at midnight on 31 December of the year preceding the year in which the competition takes place.
- Fencers taking part in all the official FIE Junior competitions, individual or team, must be under twenty years old at midnight on 31 December of the year preceding the year in which the competition takes place.

COMPETITION ORGANIZATION (ABRIDGED)

Senior Open World Championships, Open World Cup and Open Grand Prix competitions are run to what the FIE calls a Mixed Formula, generally over two days...

Day 1: The Preliminary Phase
- The sixteen fencers entered who are ranked highest in the most recent official FIE rankings are exempt from the preliminary phase.
- Using the latest official FIE rankings to seed the poules, they are drawn up to consist of as many poules of seven as possible, with remaining poules of six...
- As far as possible, fencers of the same nationality are placed in different poules.
- After the round of poules, 20 to 30 per cent of the participants... are eliminated, based on the indices of all those competing in them. For Grand Prix competitions, the number of fencers eliminated on the indices of the poules must be 30 per cent.
- After the round of poules, the sixteen fencers ranked highest are exempt from the preliminary direct elimination table.
- Based on the indices of the fencers in all the poules, the remaining fencers qualifying from the poules will make up a direct elimination table, which is fenced until only thirty-two competitors remain.
- This makes up sixty-four fencers, who compete on the following day.

Day 2: The Main Phase
...this is an L64 tableau made up of:
- Places 1-16 – The seeded fencers exempted from the preliminary phase.
- Places 17-32 – The sixteen fencers who have the highest indices after the round of poules.
- Places 33-64 – The thirty-two fencers qualifying from the preliminary direct elimination table, classified according to their indices after the round of poules.

The L64 tableau is normally fenced on four pistes... The first round of the table of sixty-four may be fenced on eight, except for Grand Prix competitions, which must be fenced on only four pistes. Junior and Cadet World Championships and Junior World Cup competitions are run on one day and consist of one qualifying round of poules where all the fencers take part, followed by a direct elimination table.

(Usher, in Paul, et al., 2012, pp.94, 96)

- Apart from these stipulations, there is no maximum age limit for those taking part in any other official events of the FIE, except in regard to the different Veteran categories. (FIE, various dates)
- Veterans are aged forty or over in the current membership year which starts on 1 January. (BVF, 2013)

The main types of competition are:

- World Championships, which can be Cadet, Junior, Senior or Veteran.
- Zonal Championships, which can be Cadet, Junior or Senior.
- World Cups (Category As and Grand Prix), which can be Junior or Senior.
- Satellite As, which are Senior.

(Usher, in Paul, et al., 2012, p.90)

More information is included in the panel entitled The International Competition Circuit.

Team competitions are attached to the World and Zonal Championship. There is also a circuit Senior Team World Cup event, usually attached to Category A or Grand Prix competitions. The Team World Cup tournament is made up of a maximum five competitions, with Team World Ranking points allocated at the end of each competition. (Usher, in Paul, et al., 2012, p.90)

Information on the running of these competitions is shown in the panel entitled Competition Organization.

'All the mental, physical and technical preparation is totally useless if your equipment fails. For a big competition you must have at least four matching weapons, all working and legal the night before the competition… Have

Observing the action at the Glasgow Open, 2014.

BECOMING A HIGH PERFORMANCE FENCER

Observing the action at the Glasgow Open, 2014.

your own tool kit, with screws, springs and points for fixing weapons with gauges, weights and test box. Always have spare bodywires.' (Kingston, 2001, p.63) Rather than rely on others to lend or fix your weapons, learn to look after them and adjust them yourself. (Kingston, 2001)

Main Points

- Fencers are likely to warm up several times during the course of a competition: each does it in his or her own way.
- It is important that you to learn to cope with stressful situations.
- Good core stability cannot be attained by fencing alone.
- Short-term fencing endurance can be assessed by how an individual reacts to fencing in a bout, mid-term endurance by fencing in a round and long-term endurance by fencing in a competition.
- Good fencing technique begins with an efficient and comfortable on guard position.
- Instinctive motor habits have to be overcome when learning technique. Speeding up too quickly can lead to false motor habits.
- Tactics are the correct application of actions in order to achieve the best possible results. Tactical lessons prepare the pupil for combat.
- In simple terms, 'reaction time' is the time it takes a fencer to perceive a simple attack and execute a single parry.
- A fencer who can discern the final line of an attack is more likely to be competent in defence.

- With 'open eyes', a fencer reacts instantly to changing circumstances.
- Failure to assess distance correctly can lead to over-lunging, lunging too short, over-extending the sword arm when hitting or finishing too close to the opponent.
- Recognizing an opening line (in modern fencing) is done mainly through visual observation. Attacking into an opening line is more effective than attacking into a line where the blade is stationary.
- Choosing an appropriate surprise action and its timing requires careful reading of the opponent.
- In order to build up national ranking points, a fencer must plan to enter a number of key competitions throughout the year.

CHAPTER SEVEN

THE SEVENTH ESSENTIAL (IN CONCLUSION)

Hold your foil as if you were holding a bird in your hand: not too hard, so as not to choke it, but at the same time hard enough, so as not to let it escape.
(Justin Lafaugère cited in Czajkowski, 2005, p.108)

The above adage was told to me as a beginner when I first learned to fence foil years ago in the school fencing club. The sport of fencing has changed a lot since then, yet helpful advice like this still has its place, particularly in the early stages of learning. These days, similar advice might include being well prepared (physically and mentally) to fence. Start by thinking about your competitions well in advance and approach them as part of a cycle of events that will lead to long-term improvements. There is no single reason for success and no one type of person who is successful. Success is both relative and fleeting. Progress towards long-term goals, not

The Camden International cadet sabre, London, 2014. (1) (Photos: Graham Morrison)

THE SEVENTH ESSENTIAL (IN CONCLUSION)

The Camden International cadet sabre, London, 2014. (1) (Photos: Graham Morrison)

THE SEVENTH ESSENTIAL (IN CONCLUSION)

separate individual achievements, is what really matters.

So far, I have been on a 'gathering mission', seeking out ideas and techniques from a variety of sources that suggest how to go about becoming a high-performance fencer. I hope that you have found this useful. Two of the fundamental forces at work in modern fencing these days are the sheer athleticism necessary to fence and the mental endurance required to endure the rigours of competition. To achieve this, fencers must foster a lifestyle that leads to physical and mental excellence, addressing weaknesses and nurturing the processes of learning for their own sakes.

Physical Fitness

These days, to be fit enough to fence at élite level you should be fit enough for life and then more. Much more. The explosive needs of high-performance fencing require in-depth physical training and, from time to time, specialist advice. Regular training brings with it regular habits and commitments, which others may see as distractions unless they are a party to your plans: players in your special drama, with all its highs and lows. With good physical training, emerging efficiency will be matched, in time, with supreme confidence. Rest is the phase when your muscles grow and strength increases. To maintain or improve such assets, it will be necessary to use them frequently.

Regular training teaches the nervous system and muscles to interact to cope with unstable situations with (at times) complex movements and to try to avoid injury. It is only when various muscles stabilize the core of the body that a fencer's limbs will perform efficiently. Improving strength and conditioning should improve performance but in fencing this in itself is no sure guarantee of success.

Physical and mental fitness go hand-in-hand. Both must be practised regularly so that their applications will be meaningful and their natures precise, resilient and used to good effect.

Mental Fitness

Precision thinking can only emanate from a supremely organized mind. Thinking is a form of training that we tend to forget about, or at least underrate. Yet, a well-prepared mind can be as important as a well-prepared body and at the serious end of the fencing spectrum, there are considerable pressures on both. Good preparation (in every respect) is the key to self-confidence.

The brain can be hardwired by consistent 'good' training and this means first making the best kinds of decisions about how you would like to improve. Improvement occurs in stages, which should lead each time to some upgrading of the status quo. A lot of 'good' thinking will occur through discussions with your coach and senior (more experienced) fencers. At the end of the day, however, everything you do on the piste, you do by yourself – here you are completely alone. A history of success in fencing competitions will hold you in good stead but you may feel, as a consequence, that you have something to live up to. A newcomer may be glad simply not to be eliminated at an important competition and, with no reputation to protect, feel less inhibited. Perhaps you were that beginner once yourself.

Effective tactics require a mental agility that allows a fencer to solve problems during the course of a bout, or (even better) before, by careful observations on an opponent's weaknesses; and in this, your coach, as an observer

THE SEVENTH ESSENTIAL (IN CONCLUSION)

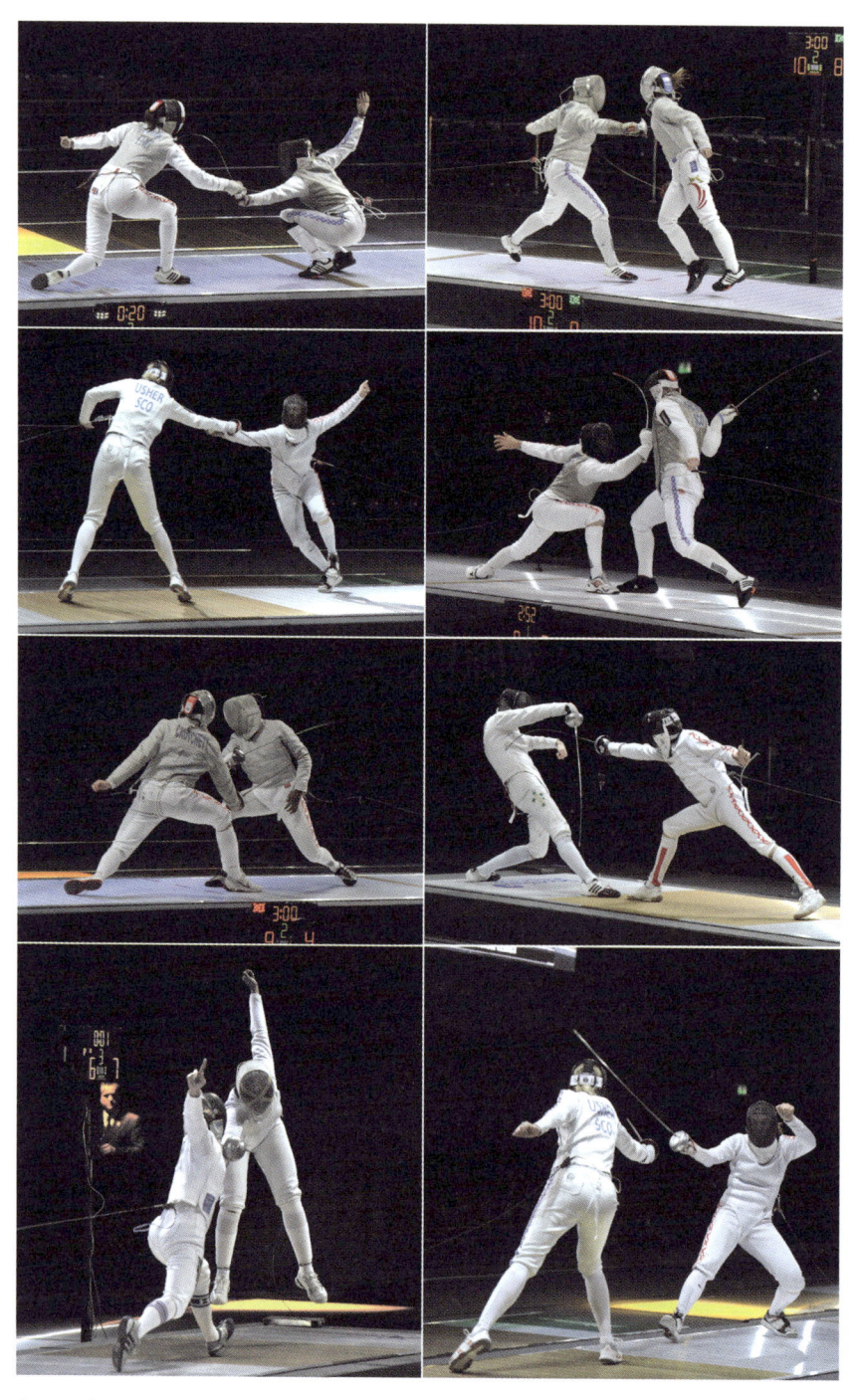

Assorted photographs from the Commonwealth Fencing Championships, Largs, 2014.

THE SEVENTH ESSENTIAL (IN CONCLUSION)

and fellow traveller, has an important role to play.

Sports Nutrition

In the world of fencing athleticism, food is fuel and the correct hydration of the body is essential. The proper consumption of nutrients is part of the lifestyle a serious sportsperson must adopt in order to train and compete successfully. This includes developing an awareness of how the body works when fencing and exercising, as well as its nutritional needs within these cycles. A basic understanding of the underlying principles is all that is required.

High Performance

Great fencers are unlikely to be born that way. They tend to make their way through regular application and consistent, heuristic endeavour, over extended periods of time. Here, failure is simply something to pass through on the way to a better learning experience. There is transience in defeat but there is also transience in winning. 'Best' is usually a 'next' or 'future' experience that, once attained, is sought again under new terms. Difficult training tasks that others shy away from must be pursued rigorously and conquered. It is only by setting challenging goals that fencers will tend to exceed their (perceived) limitations. Past successes provide a compelling repertoire of strokes that may be difficult to ignore. Yet if we relive our successes too often, their effectiveness will diminish.

The extent of time required to train to world-class performance levels in many fields has been estimated at 10,000 hours. There must be important underlying reasons why some people are prepared to commit so much time and energy to this type of endeavour.

The Seventh Essential

At the outset, I suggested that the 'seventh essential' in a high-performance fencer's mind is how to prepare him/herself physically and mentally to fence. Such hard endeavour can take a fencer to the point of excellence, even from modest beginnings. Early talent may seem encouraging but for those who do not experience fencing in this way, the struggle begins early. For them, training (preparation) in all its forms becomes a regular occurrence. Those who do succeed seem to have a compelling need to do so. They are able to attune their physical and mental processes to perform when it really matters. The reason why this happens is less important than the fact that such abilities do exist. Any reason that works as an efficient trigger for this should deliver the required results.

So, find that reason if you can – your reason – for in doing so, you will truly discover your own seventh essential.

GLOSSARY

accelerating lunge where the sword arm is held back waiting for an explosive finish (Borysiuk, 2009)

aerobic capacity the maximum rate at which the body can make use of oxygen per minute (Friedberg, 1984)

aerobic threshold the level of effort at which anaerobic energy pathways start to be a significant part of energy production (Barder, 2002)

amino acids basic components of all proteins (Dunford and Doyle, 2008)

anaerobic threshold the level of exercise intensity at which lactic acid builds up in the body faster than it can be cleared away (Barder, 2002)

antibodies specialised cells of the immune system that fight infections (Medical-Dictionary, n.d.)

anticipatory reaction a motor response made after anticipating the speed and path of a moving object (SSTT, 2011)

antioxidants man-made or natural substances that may prevent or delay some types of cell damage (U.S. National Library of Medicine, 2014)

attaques-au-fer attacks on the blade (SSTT, 2011)

autonomic nervous system contains nerves that control bodily processes (Encarta Dictionary: English (U.K.), n.d.)

calories a measure of the amount of energy in food (NHS Choices, 2012 – b)

capillaries are extremely small blood vessels that transport blood from arteries to veins (Bailey, n.d.)

cardiovascular system the organic system that allows blood to circulate, nutrients to be transported and waste products removed (Wikipedia, n.d. – a)

centring a simple breathing technique to reduce tension and increase relaxation (Kogler, 2005)

choice reaction a motor response that varies according to the stimulus given (SSTT, 2011)

circuit training where a set for each exercise is performed once every cycle (Winch, 2004)

circulatory system see cardiovascular system

GLOSSARY

compound reaction may be composed of one or more choice, differential, anticipatory and intuitive reactions (SSTT, 2011)

concentric contraction where the muscle gets shorter (James, 2006)

conditioned reflex a reflex response to a new stimulus that can be learned (BBC, n.d.)

conditioning the work needed to prepare for the stresses and strains of specific training and competition (Winch, 2005)

core stability keeping the correct posture during athletic performance (Winch, 2005)

counter-time a tactic that consists of provoking an offensive or counter-offensive reaction so it can be opposed with a riposte or attack (Gaugler, 1997)

deliberate practice where certain sharply defined elements of performance are identified for improvement then practised intensely (Colvin, 2010)

developmental stretch after the easy stretch, push a little further (Anderson, 1981)

differential reaction a motor response to only one selected stimulus (SSTT, 2011)

direct elimination where winners are promoted (at a competition) and losers eliminated after one fight (BF, n.d.)

diuretic increases urine extraction of water and electrolytes (Patient.co.uk., n.d.)

dynamic strength a type of strength that relates to a type of movement (Winch, 2004)

easy stretch stretching initially to the point where you feel a mild tension (Anderson, 1981)

eccentric contraction where the muscle lengthens (James, 2006)

electrolytes mineral salts dissolved in the body's fluid that conduct an electrical current (Kleiner and Greenwood-Robinson, 1996)

enzymes protein molecules in cells that speed up chemical reactions in the body without being used up in the process (Simple Wikipedia, 2014)

extrinsic motivation something you do because you have to (Czajkowski, 2005)

fencing line an imaginary line between two fencers that runs through their heels and the toes of the leading foot (Gaugler, 1997)

FIE Fédération Internationale d'Escrime

fixed mindset a belief that your abilities are natural characteristics (Sportscotland. n.d.)

flanconade an attack directed against the flank of an opponent (SSTT, 2002)

full mobility the maximum range of movement in a joint (Winch, 2005)

general strength endurance the ability to move a resistance for prolonged periods (Winch, 2004)

glucose any of several forms of naturally occurring sugar (Higgleton, *et al.*, 2001)

GLOSSARY

glycogen a storage form of glucose found in the muscles and liver (Hazeldine, 1985)

growth mindset a belief that your abilities are characteristics that can be developed (Sportscotland. n.d.)

heart rate the number of times the heart beats per minute (Hazeldine, 1985)

hormones chemical messengers that are secreted directly into the blood (Mandal, 2014 – a)

hypertonic sports drink contains a greater number of particles per 100ml than the body's own fluids (Bean, 2009)

hyperventilate over-breathe (Kogler, 2005)

hypotonic sports drink contains a smaller number of particles per 100ml than the body's own fluids (Bean, 2009)

ideomotor training where an athlete visualizes a clear picture of the task ahead and achieves self-control (Kogler, 2005)

intrinsic motivation something you do because it is pleasant or satisfying (Czajkowski, 2005)

intrinsic speed the speed with which you were born (Winch, 2004)

intuitive reaction a motor response based on intuition, not conscious thought (SSTT, 2011)

isometric exercise when the muscle does not change length (Wyrick, 1971)

isotonic exercise when the muscle changes length (Wyrick, 1971)

isotonic sports drink contains about the same number of particles per 100ml as the body's own fluids (Bean, 2009)

local strength endurance the ability to perform prolonged work against resistance in a localized area of the body (Winch, 2004)

maltodextrin a proprietary carbohydrate derived from starch (Wikipedia, n.d. – b)

metabolism refers to all the physical and chemical processes in the body that convert or use energy (Dugdale and Zieve, 2012)

micronutrients essential dietary elements that are needed in very small amounts (Medical-Dictionary, n.d.)

minerals essential nutrients the body needs in small amounts to function properly (NHS Choices, 2012 – a)

mobility the range of movement allowed by the joints (Winch 2005)

motor adaptability the ability to adapt fencing actions in unpredictable situations (Prof. Zbigniew Czajkowski, cited in SSTT, 2011, p.116)

motor control the ability to direct one's movements precisely (Prof. Zbigniew Czajkowski, cited in SSTT, 2011, p.116)

motor educability the ability to learn new strokes and change old motor habits (Prof. Zbigniew Czajkowski, cited in SSTT, 2011, p.116)

GLOSSARY

motor response a reaction to a known stimulus (Czajkowski, 2005)

nervous system a complex network of nerves and cells that carry messages to and from the brain and spinal cord to various parts of the body (Mandal, 2014 – b)

open eyes an attack that commences without premeditation of the opponent's response and adapts accordingly (Smith, 2003)

over-learning a teaching method attributed to Jean Louis de Montpellier (cited in Czajkowski, 2005, p.130–131).

overload developing strength by making muscles work with a little more load than they can cope with comfortably (Wyrick, 1971)

perceived exertion how hard a workout feels (Waterson, 2003)

periodization planning training sessions in an organized manner

plyometrics involves the prior rapid stretching of the muscle before contraction. (Winch, 2004)

poules (sometimes spelled 'pools') are run at the beginning of a competition to rank all fencers for the eventual direct elimination (Paul, et al., 2012)

prises-de-fer takings of the blade (SSTT, 2011)

proprioception the ability of the brain to sense the position of a joint or how the body is positioned (Esteves, et al., 2015)

protein a basic component of a living cell (Borysiuk, 2009)

reaction time the interval between stimulus and response (Tau, 2005)

self-talk the things that an individual says to himself or herself mentally (Encarta Dictionary: English (U.K.), n.d.)

set a term used for a group of repetitions in exercise (Winch, 2004)

simple reaction is the reaction to a known stimulus with a known motor response (SSTT, 2011)

smart muscle the ability of muscle to deal with unstable situations (James, 2006)

specificity choosing exercises that are relevant to the requirements of a particular sport (Hazeldine and Cadman, 1984)

speed the time taken to coordinate the movement of individual joints or the body as a whole (Hazeldine and Cadman, 1984)

split routine where specific muscle groups are worked on different days, allowing sufficient recovery time for each group (Hazeldine and Cadman, 1984)

stage training where sets for each exercise are all performed consecutively (Winch, 2004)

static strength the application of force against a non-moving resistance (Winch, 2004)

GLOSSARY

strength the maximum force which a muscle, or group of muscles, can generate against a resistance (Hazeldine and Cadman, 1984)

suppleness the range of movement allowed by the muscle-tendon soft tissue structures (Winch 2005)

tactics the correct application of actions in order to achieve the best possible results (SSTT, 2011)

training cycles see periodization

training effect the benefits of training that are lost if training stops (Norris, 1994)

training maturity the number of years an athlete has been training for their sport (Shepherd, 2006)

vitamins essential nutrients the body needs in small amounts to function properly (NHS Choices, 2012 – a)

weight training exercising with light weights using a high number of repetitions

REFERENCES

Alaux, M., 1975. *Modern Fencing: Foil, Épée, and Sabre*. New York: Charles Scribner's Sons.

American College of Sports Medicine (ACSM). 2003. *ACSM Fitness Book: A Proven Step-by-Step Program from the Experts*. 3rd ed. Champaign, IL: Human Kinetics.

Anderson, B., 1973. *Better Fencing-Foil*. London: Kaye and Ward.

Anderson, B., 1981. *Stretching: Exercises for Everyday Fitness and for Twenty-Five Individual Sports*. London: Pelham Books.

Bailey, R., 2014, *Capillary*. Available at; www.biology.about.com/od/anatomy/ss/capillaryhtm.

Bakker, A.E, *et al.*, 2011. 'Flow and performance: A study among talented Dutch soccer players.' *Psychology of Sport and Exercise*, 1–9, p.7.

Bandrei, R., 2012. *Fencing Basics: All About Fencing*. Milton Keynes: Amazon.co.uk, Ltd.

Barder, O., 2002. *Running for Fitness*. London: A and C Black.

Barraclough, J., 2013. *Amateurs vs. Experts*. Available at: www.thesportinmind.com/articles/amateurs-vs-experts

Barth, Prof. B. and Beck, E., eds., 2007. *The Complete Guide to Fencing*. UK: Meyer and Meyer Sport (UK) Ltd.

BBC, 2014. *Reflex Responses*. Available at: www.bbc.co.uk/schools/gcsebitesize/science/add_ocr_21c/brain_mind/reflexresponsesrev1.shtml

Bean, A., 2002. *Food for Fitness*. 2nd ed. London: A and C Black.

Bean, A., 2003. *Fitness on a Plate*. London: A and C Black.

Bean, A., 2009. *The Complete Guide to Sports Nutrition*. 6th ed. London: A and C Black.

de Beaumont, C.-L., 1954. *Fencing – Foyles Handbooks*. London: W. and G. Foyle Ltd.

de Beaumont, C.-L., 1968. *Fencing*. London: The English Universities Press Ltd.

de Beaumont, C.-L., 1978. *All About Fencing: Foil, Épée, Sabre*. Toronto: Coles Publishing Co.

Beke, Z. and Polgár, J., 1963. *The Methodology of Sabre Fencing*. Budapest: Corvina Press.

Benson, C., 2012. *Performance +: The Performance and Nutritional Guide for Athletes*. Available at: www.sportscotland.org.uk/media/719807/Performance-plus-2012-final.pdf

REFERENCES

Binet, A., (Heisler, S., trans.), 1975 (original work 1911). *Modern Ideas About Children*. Menlo Park, CA: Suzanne Heisler.

Borysiuk, Z., 2009. *Modern Saber Fencing: Technique-Tactics-Training-Research*. Staten Island, NY: SKA Swordplay Books.

Bower, M., 1997. *Foil Fencing*. 8th ed. USA: McGraw-Hill.

British Fencing (BF), n.d. *Glossary of Terms*. Available at: www.britishfencing.com/about-fencing/glossary_of_terms

British Fencing (BF). 2013a. *Eden Cup 2013 Results*. Available at: www.britishfencing.com/uploads/files/eden_cup16tofinalcomplete.htm

British Fencing (BF). 2013b. *Leon Paul Cup 2013 Results*. Available at: www.britishfencing.com/uploads/files/leon_paul_satellite-116_to_final.htm

British Veterans Fencing (BVF), 2013. *BVF Constitution*. Available at: www.veterans-fencing.co.uk/documents/constitution.pdf

Brown, M. and Adamson, J., 1995. *The Flexibility Factor: A Complete Guide to Flexibility in Sport*. London: Pelham Books.

Campos, J., 1988. *The Art of Fencing: Foil, Épée, Sabre*. New York: Vantage Press Inc.

CNN, 2008. *Grand Spectacle Closes Beijing's Olympics*. Available at: www.edition.cnn.com/2008/SPORT/08/24/olympics.close

Cochrane, N., 2012. *Performance +: The Performance and Nutritional Guide for Athletes*. Available at: www.sportscotland.org.uk/media/719807/Performance-plus-2012-final.pdf

Coggan, A.R. and Coyle, E.F., 1987. 'Reversal of fatigue during prolonged exercise by carbohydrate infusion or ingestion', *J. Appl. Physiol.*, vol 63, pp.2388–95.

Colvin, G., 2010. *Talent is Overrated: What Really Separates World-Class Performers from Everybody Else*. London: Nicholas Brealey Publishing.

Connaughton, D., et al., 2008. 'The development and maintenance of mental toughness: Perceptions of élite performers.' *Journal of Sport Sciences*, 26, 83–95, cited in Crust, p.45.

Coyle, D., 2010. 'Fight Club: Is Talent Taught Rather Than Innate?' *Eureka* (Times Magazine), May, p49.

Cross, T. and Kirkham, E., 1996. *Introduction to Fencing*. Champaign, IL: Stipes Publishing.

Czajkowski, Dr. Z., 2005. *Understanding Fencing: The Unity of Theory and Practice*. Staten Island, NY: SKA Swordplay Books.

Dugdale, Prof. D.C. and Zieve, Dr. D., 2012. *Metabolism*. Available at: www.ncbi.nlm.nih.gov/pubmedhealth/PMH0002917/

Dunford, M. and Doyle, J.A., 2008. *Nutrition for Sport and Exercise*. 2nd ed. Belmont, CA: Wadsworth.

Dunford, M., 2010. *Fundamentals of Sport and Exercise Nutrition*. Champaign, IL: Human Kinetics.

Dweck, Dr. C.S., 2007. *Mindset: How You Can Fulfil Your Potential*. London: Constable and Robinson Ltd.

REFERENCES

Encarta Dictionary: English (U.K.), n.d. Microsoft Word (Non-Commercial Use).

Ericsson, K.A., Krampe, R.T, and Tesch-Romer, C., 1993. 'The Role of Deliberate Practice in the Acquisition of Expert Performance'. *Psychological Review*, Vol. 100, No. 3, pp.363-406. www.projects.ict.usc.edu/itw/gel/EricssonDeliberatePracticePR93.pdf

Esteves, J., *et al.*, 2015. 'Lateral and Postural Asymmetries in Fencing'. *The Sword*, January, 2015

Fédération Internationale d'Escrime (FIE.), various dates. *Rules*. Available at: www.fie.ch/Fencing/Rules.aspx

Friedberg, A., 1984. *The Facts on File Dictionary of Fitness*. New York: Facts on File Publications.

Gardner, H., 1997. *Extraordinary Minds*. New York: Basic Books.

Garret, M.R., Kaidanov, E.G. and Pezza, G.A., 1995. *Foil, Saber and Épée Fencing: Skills, Safety, Operations, and Responsibilities*. 2nd ed. Penn State: The Pennsylvania State University Press.

Gaugler, Maestro W.M., 1997. *A Dictionary of Universally Used Fencing Terminology*. Bangor, Maine: Laureate Press.

Gisolphi, C.V., *et al.*,1992. 'Intestinal water absorption from select carbohydrate solutions in humans', *J. Appl. Physiol.*, vol 73, pp.2142–50.

Gladwell, M., 2008. *Outliers: The Story of Success*. London: Allen Lane.

Griffin, J., 2002. *Food for Sport: Eat Well, Perform Better*. Ramsbury, Wilts: The Crowood Press Ltd.

Gunnell, S., 2001. *Be Your Best: How Anyone Can Become Fit, Healthy and Confident*. London: Thorsons.

Harmenberg, J., *et al.*, 2007. *Epee 2.0: The Birth of the New Fencing Paradigm*. Staten Island, NY: SKA Swordplay Books.

Harvard School of Public Health (HSPH), 2014. *Omega-3 Fatty Acids: An essential Contribution*. Available at: hsph.harvard.edu/nutritionsource/omega-3-fats

Hazeldine, R., 1985. *Fitness for Sport*. Ramsbury, Wilts: The Crowood Press Ltd.

Hazeldine, R. and Cadman, J., 1984. *The Body in Action*. Leeds: The National Coaching Foundation.

Hett, G. V., 1951. *Fencing*. London: Sir Isaac Pitman and Sons Ltd.

Higgleton, E., *et al.*, 2001. *The Chambers Dictionary*. Edinburgh: Chambers Harrap Publishers Ltd.

Holt, Dr. S., 2004. *Fitness Food: The Essential Guide to Eating Well and Performing Better*. Millers Point, NSW: Murdoch Books Australia.

International Association of Athletic Federations (IAAF), 2007. *Nutrition for Athletics: The 2007 IAAF Consensus Statement*.

James, H., 2006. *Strength Training for Fencers*. Staten Island, NY: SKA Swordplay Books.

REFERENCES

Kerr, P., 2014. *Nutrition for Exercise*. Available at: www.bupa.co.uk/individuals/health-information/directory/n/nutrition-for-exercise#textBlock224031

Kingston, T., 2001, *Epée Combat Manual*. London: Terrence Kingston.

Kleiner, S.M. and Greenwood-Robinson, M., 1996. *High Performance Nutrition: The Total Eating Plan to Maximize Your Workout*. New York: John Wiley and Sons, Inc.

Knapp, B., 1970. *Skills in Sport: The Attainment of Proficiency*. London: Routledge and K. Paul.

Kogler, A., 2005. *One Touch at a Time: Psychological Processes in Fencing*. 2nd ed. Staten Island: NY: SKA Swordplay Books.

Levitin, D., 2006. *This Is Your Brain on Music: Understanding a Human Obsession*. London: Atlantic Books Ltd.

Lukovich, I., 1998. *Fencing: The Modern International Style*. Staten Island, NY: SKA Swordplay Books.

Lukovich, I., 2013. *Foil Fencing: Technique, Tactics, and Training (A Manual for Coaches and Coaching Candidates)*. Staten Island, NY: SKA Swordplay Books.

Mandal, Dr, A., 2014 – a. *What are Hormones?* Available at: www.news-medical.net/health/What-are-Hormones.aspx

Mandal, Dr. A., 2014 – b. *What is the Nervous System?* Available at: www.news-medical.net/health/What-is-the-Nervous-System.aspx

Manley, A., 1979. *Complete Fencing: A Definitive Guide to the Sport*. London: Robert Hale Ltd.

Manore, M.M., Meyer, N.L. and Thompson, J., 2009. *Sport Nutrition for Health and Performance*. 2nd ed. Champaign, IL: Human Kinetics.

Medical-Dictionary, 2014. *Antibodies*. Available at: www.medical-dictionary.thefreedictionary.com/antibodies

Medical-Dictionary, n.d., *Micronutrients*. Available at: www.medical-dictionary.thefreedictionary.com/Micronutrients [Accessed 30 July 2014]

Morehouse, T. and Sundem, G., 2012. *American Fencer: Modern Lessons from an Ancient Sport*. Boston, MA: Acanthus Publishers.

Morgan, D., 2007. *Be Your Best: The Smart Way to Improve Your Body, Shape and Mind*. London: Virgin Books Ltd.

Mueller, C.M. and Dweck, C.S., 1998. 'Praise for Intelligence Can Undermine Children's Motivation and Performance'. *Journal of Personal and Social Psychology*, Vol. 75, No. 1, pp.33–52. www.uky.edu/~eushe2/mrg/MuellerDweck1998.pdf

Muliar, D., 2001. *Fitness Food*. Stroud: Gaia Books Ltd.

NHS Choices, 2012 – a. *Vitamins and Minerals*. www.nhs.uk/Conditions/vitamins-minerals/Pages/Vitamins-minerals.aspx

NHS Choices, 2012 – b. *Understanding Calories*. Available at: www.nhs.uk/Livewell/loseweight/Pages/understanding-calories.aspx

Norcross, T., 1978. *Fencing the Foil*. London: Ward Lock Ltd.

REFERENCES

Norris, C.M., 1994. *Flexibility: Principles and Practice*. London: A and C Black.

Olympic Movement, 2008, *Sabre Team Men*. Available at: www.olympic.org/fencing-sabre-team-men

Paterson, C., 2012. *Performance +: The Performance and Nutritional Guide for Athletes*. Available at: www.sportscotland.org.uk/media/719807/Performance-plus-2012-final.pdf

Patient.co.uk., n.d. *Diuretics*. Available at: www.patient.co.uk/doctor/Diuretics

Paul, Prof. S, et al., 2012. *Épée Fencing: A Step-by-Step Guide to Achieving Olympic Gold*. UK: Wellard Publishing.

Pitman, B., 1988. *Fencing: Techniques of Foil, Épée and Sabre*. Ramsbury, Wilts: The Crowood Press Ltd.

Roberts, D., 2011. 'The Influence of Proprioceptive Exercises on Lower Limb Balance of Football Players'. s.n.

Robinson, B., n.d. *Progression and Regression of the Back Squat*. Available at: www.healthyliving.azcentral.com/progressions-regressions-back-squat-4108.html

Rogers, E., 2013. *Advanced Fencing Techniques: Discussions with Bert Bracewell*. Ramsbury, Wilts: The Crowood Press Ltd.

Shaff, J., 1982. *Fencing*. New York: Atheneum.

Shepherd, J., 2006. *Sports Training*. London: A and C Black.

Shirreffs, S.M., et al., 1996. 'Post-exercise rehydration in man: effects of volume consumed and drink sodium content.' *Med. Sci. Sports Ex.*, vol 28, pp.1260–71.

Shirreffs, S.M., et al., 2004. 'Fluid and electrolyte needs for preparation and recovery from training and competition.' *J. Sports Sci.* Vol 22, pp.57–63.

Simmonds, Prof. A.T. and Morton, E.D., 1997. *Fencing to Win*. London: The Sportsman's Press.

Simple Wikipedia, 2014. *Enzyme*. Available at: www.simple.wikipedia.org/wiki/Enzyme

Sly, B., 2014. Eating to recover: *How and What to Eat Post Workout*. Available at: www.breakingmuscle.com/mobility-recovery/eating-to-recover-how-and-what-to-eat-post-workout

Smith, Prof. J.E., 2003. *Foil Fencing: The Techniques and Tactics of Modern Foil Fencing*. Chichester, West Sussex: Summersdale Publishers Ltd.

Sportscotland. n.d. *Mindset*. Available at: www.sportscotland.org.uk/media/734909/Mindset-Information-sheet.pdf

Standing Sub-Committee for Technique and Terminology (SSTT), 2002. *Summary of Fencing Theory and Terminology*. British Academy of Fencing.

Standing Sub-Committee for Technique and Terminology (SSTT), 2011. *A Compendium of the Theory and Practice of Teaching and Coaching Fencing*. British Academy of Fencing.

REFERENCES

Stöckel, T. and Weigelt, M., 2012. 'Brain lateralisation and motor learning: Selective effects of dominant and non-dominant hand practice on the early acquisition of throwing skills'. *Laterality: Asymmetries of Body, Brain and Cognition*, 17(1), pp.18–37.

Syed, M., 2010. *Bounce: How Champions Are Made*. London: Fourth Estate.

Tau, B.H., 2005. *Fencing Volume One, Competitive Training and Practice*. New York: Wysteria Publishing.

Track and Field Coach, n.d. *Periodization Made Simple*. Available at: trackandfieldcoach.ca

U.S. National Library of Medicine, 2014. *Antioxidants*. Available at: www.nlm.nih.gov/medlineplus/antioxidants.html

Verstegen, M. and Williams, P., 2005. *Core Performance Essentials*. London: Rodale International Ltd.

Volkmann, Dr. R., 1997. *Magnum Libre d'Escrime (Big Book of Fencing)*. 2nd ed. Augusta, GA: Volkmann.

Waterson, S., 2003. Body Challenge: *30-Minutes-a Day*. London: Thorsons.

Whyte, Prof. G., 2012. 'The Future of Sport: Natural Born Winners?' *The Guardian* Available at: www.sportscotland.org.uk/media/701946/natural-born-winners.pdf.

Wikipedia, 2014 – a. *Circulatory System*. Available at: www.en.wikipedia.org/wiki/Circulatory_system

Wikipedia, 2014 – b. *Maltodextrin*. Available at: www.en.wikipedia.org/wiki/Maltodextrin

Winch, M. A., 2004. *Strength Training for Athletes*. Ramsbury, Wilts: The Crowood Press Ltd.

Winch, M. A., 2005, *Conditioning for Athletes*. Ramsbury, Wilts: The Crowood Press Ltd.

Winner, Prof. E., 2010. 'Fight Club: Is Talent Taught Rather Than Innate?' *Eureka* (Times Magazine), May, p49.

Wojciechowski, Z., n.d. *Theory, Methods and Exercises in Fencing*. London: Amateur Fencing Association.

Wyrick, W., 1971. *Foil Fencing*. Philadelphia, PA: W. B. Saunders Company.

INDEX

A
accelerating lunge   113
aerobic capacity   32
aerobic threshold   32
amino acids   63, 74
anaerobic threshold   32
antibodies   63
anticipatory reaction   118, 119, 120
antioxidants   72
attaques-au-fer   114
autonomic nervous system   98

B
Bracewell, Prof. H.T.   8, 114, 122, 123

C
calories   60
capillaries   45
cardiovascular system   37
centring   103
choice reaction   118, 118, 120
circuit training   30
circulatory system   29
compound reaction   119
concentric contraction   51, 58
conditioned reflex   47
conditioning   6, 8, 13, 30, 35, 36, 37, 58, 96, 143
core stability   37, 38, 41, 44, 58, 113, 139
counter-time   118, 118, 126, 133

D
deliberate practice   10, 84, 85, 87
developmental stretch   20, 33
differential reaction   117, 118
direct elimination   18, 72, 137
diuretic   71
dynamic strength   46, 47, 58

E
easy stretch   20, 26, 33
eccentric contraction   51, 58
electrolytes   64, 65
enzymes   30, 60, 63, 78
extrinsic motivation   99

F
fencing line   113
fixed mindset   85, 86, 87
flanconade   116
full mobility   46

G
general strength endurance   47, 58
glucose   62, 68, 71
glycogen   32, 64, 68, 71, 74
growth mindset   85, 86, 87

H
heart rate   30, 32, 37
hormones   63, 68

INDEX

hypertonic sports drink   65
hyperventilate   103
hypotonic sports drink   65

I
ideomotor training   106
intrinsic motivation   99
intrinsic speed   17
intuitive reaction   117, 118
isometric exercise   29, 33
isotonic exercise   29, 33
isotonic sports drink   64, 65, 66, 71

L
local strength endurance   47, 58

M
maltodextrin   77
metabolism   19, 30, 32, 37, 60, 68
micronutrients   74
minerals   60, 64, 67, 72
mobility   17, 36, 37, 41, 45, 46, 96, 117
de Montpellier, J., L.   99
Morehouse, T.   10
motor adaptability   114
motor control   114
motor educability   114
motor response   117

N
nervous system   17, 29, 45, 50, 60, 74, 98, 99, 143

O
open eyes   118, 120, 125, 139
over-learning   99
overload   29, 30, 33

P
perceived exertion   30, 32
periodization   132
physical fitness   15, 33, 43, 99, 143
plyometrics   47, 51, 58
poules   15, 72, 136, 137
prises-de-fer   114, 117, 120, 128
protein   17, 29, 32, 60, 62, 63, 67, 68, 74

R
reaction time   45, 58, 114, 115, 116, 117, 118, 123, 124, 125, 126, 127, 128, 129
Rogers, J.   10

S
self-talk   101, 103, 108
set   30, 31
simple reaction   117
Simmonds, Prof. A.   123
smart muscle   35, 47
Smart, K.   10
specificity   31
speed   7, 10, 14, 15, 17, 18, 19, 20, 30, 31, 33, 36, 37, 45, 47, 58, 78, 96, 113, 114, 115, 116, 117, 118, 119, 125, 126, 131, 132, 136, 139
split routine   31
stage training   30
static strength   486
strength   6, 7, 8, 9, 15, 17, 20, 23, 29, 30, 31, 33, 35, 36, 41, 43, 45, 46, 47, 48, 53, 58, 60, 63, 64, 65, 78, 99, 111, 112, 113, 136
suppleness   17, 37, 41

T
tactics   7, 10, 96, 97, 98, 100, 101, 102, 109, 113, 114, 115, 139, 140, 143

training cycles 134
training effect 30
training maturity 17, 107

V
vitamins 60, 62, 67, 72, 74

W
weight training 29, 30, 31, 36, 38, 58
Williams, J. 10

Y
Yakimenko, A. 10

OTHER RELATED TITLES FROM CROWOOD

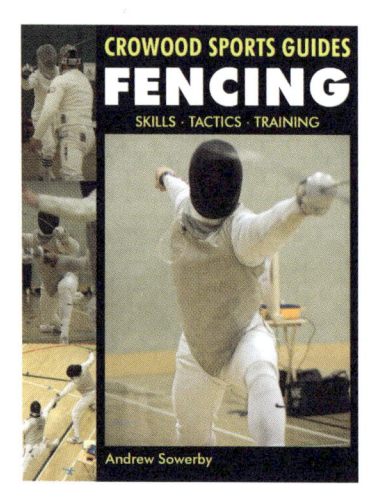

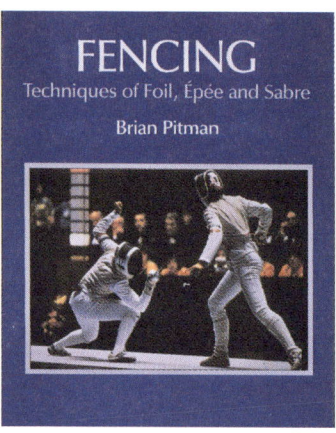

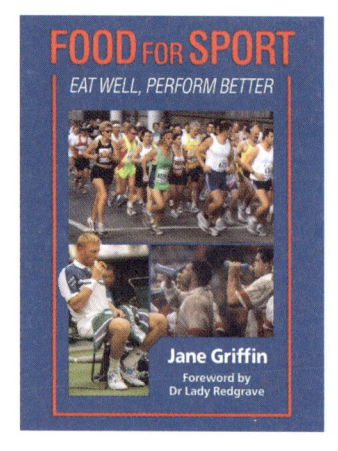

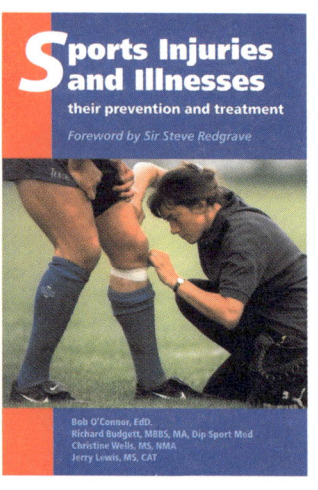